PANZER WEDGE

VOLUME ONE

The Stackpole Military History Series

THE AMERICAN CIVIL WAR
Cavalry Raids of the Civil War
Ghost, Thunderbolt, and Wizard
In the Lion's Mouth
Pickett's Charge
Witness to Gettysburg

WORLD WAR I
Doughboy War

WORLD WAR II
After D-Day
Airborne Combat
Armor Battles of the Waffen-SS,
    1943–45
Armoured Guardsmen
Army of the West
Arnhem 1944
Australian Commandos
The B-24 in China
Backwater War
The Battle of France
The Battle of Sicily
Battle of the Bulge, Vol. 1
Battle of the Bulge, Vol. 2
Beyond the Beachhead
Beyond Stalingrad
The Black Bull
Blitzkrieg Unleashed
Blossoming Silk against the
    Rising Sun
Bodenplatte
The Brandenburger Commandos
The Brigade
Bringing the Thunder
The Canadian Army and the
    Normandy Campaign
Coast Watching in World War II
Colossal Cracks
Condor
A Dangerous Assignment
D-Day Bombers
D-Day Deception
D-Day to Berlin
Decision in the Ukraine
Destination Normandy
Dive Bomber!
A Drop Too Many
Eagles of the Third Reich
The Early Battles of Eighth Army
Eastern Front Combat
Europe in Flames
Exit Rommel
The Face of Courage
Fist from the Sky
Flying American Combat Aircraft of
    World War II
For Europe
Forging the Thunderbolt
For the Homeland

Fortress France
The German Defeat in the East,
    1944–45
German Order of Battle, Vol. 1
German Order of Battle, Vol. 2
German Order of Battle, Vol. 3
The Germans in Normandy
Germany's Panzer Arm in
    World War II
GI Ingenuity
Goodwood
The Great Ships
Grenadiers
Guns against the Reich
Hitler's Nemesis
Hold the Westwall
Infantry Aces
In the Fire of the Eastern Front
Iron Arm
Iron Knights
Japanese Army Fighter Aces
JG 26 Luftwaffe Fighter Wing
    War Diary, Vol. 1
JG 26 Luftwaffe Fighter Wing
    War Diary, Vol. 2
Kampfgruppe Peiper at the Battle
    of the Bulge
The Key to the Bulge
Knight's Cross Panzers
Kursk
Luftwaffe Aces
Luftwaffe Fighter Ace
Luftwaffe Fighter-Bombers over
    Britain
Luftwaffe Fighters and Bombers
Massacre at Tobruk
Mechanized Juggernaut or Military
    Anachronism?
Messerschmitts over Sicily
Michael Wittmann, Vol. 1
Michael Wittmann, Vol. 2
Mission 376
Mountain Warriors
The Nazi Rocketeers
Night Flyer / Mosquito Pathfinder
No Holding Back
On the Canal
Operation Mercury
Packs On!
Panzer Aces
Panzer Aces II
Panzer Aces III
Panzer Commanders of the
    Western Front
Panzergrenadier Aces
Panzer Gunner
The Panzer Legions
Panzers in Normandy
Panzers in Winter
Panzer Wedge

The Path to Blitzkrieg
Penalty Strike
Poland Betrayed
Red Road from Stalingrad
Red Star under the Baltic
Retreat to the Reich
Rommel's Desert Commanders
Rommel's Desert War
Rommel's Lieutenants
The Savage Sky
Ship-Busters
The Siege of Küstrin
The Siegfried Line
A Soldier in the Cockpit
Soviet Blitzkrieg
Stalin's Keys to Victory
Surviving Bataan and Beyond
T-34 in Action
Tank Tactics
Tigers in the Mud
Triumphant Fox
The 12th SS, Vol. 1
The 12th SS, Vol. 2
Twilight of the Gods
Typhoon Attack
The War against Rommel's
    Supply Lines
War in the Aegean
War of the White Death
Winter Storm
Wolfpack Warriors
Zhukov at the Oder

THE COLD WAR / VIETNAM
Cyclops in the Jungle
Expendable Warriors
Fighting in Vietnam
Flying American Combat Aircraft:
    The Cold War
Here There Are Tigers
Land with No Sun
MiGs over North Vietnam
Phantom Reflections
Street without Joy
Through the Valley
Two One Pony

WARS OF AFRICA AND THE MIDDLE EAST
Never-Ending Conflict
The Rhodesian War

GENERAL MILITARY HISTORY
Carriers in Combat
Cavalry from Hoof to Track
Desert Battles
Guerrilla Warfare
Ranger Dawn
Sieges
The Spartan Army

PANZER WEDGE
VOLUME ONE

The German 3rd Panzer Division and the
Summer of Victory in the East

Lt. Fritz Lucke,
with Robert Edwards and Michael Olive

STACKPOLE
BOOKS

English translation © 2012 by Battle Born Books and Consulting

Published in 2012 by
STACKPOLE BOOKS
5067 Ritter Road
Mechanicsburg, PA 17055
www.stackpolebooks.com

Printed in the United States of America

10 9 8 7 6 5 4 3 2 1

Library of Congress Cataloging-in-Publication Data

Lucke, Fritz.
  [Panzerkeil im Osten. English]
  Panzer wedge / Fritz Lucke ; with Robert Edwards and Michael Olive.
    p. cm.
  Translation of: Panzerkeil im Osten : Gedenkbuch der Berlin-mdrkischen Panzer-division. Berlin : Verlag "Die Wehrmacht, 1942.
  ISBN 978-0-8117-1082-4
  1. Lucke, Fritz. 2. Germany. Heer. Panzer-Division, 3. 3. World War, 1939–1945—Personal narratives, German. 4. World War, 1939–1945—Regimental histories—Germany. 5. World War, 1939–1945—Campaigns—Eastern Front. 6. World War, 1939–1945—Tank warfare. I. Edwards, Robert. II. Olive, Michael. III. Title.
  D757.563rd L8313 2012
  940.54'1343—dc23
                              2012032603

Contents

Foreword

MY SON
The track still run in the dirt, where you went.
My gaze still follows—the gate, however, is empty.
I still feel the warmth of your cheek
When the parting words were said: Until the next time!

Goodbye, my boy. I still had something to say . . .
Yes, but what was it? I no longer know any more.
My heart returns to your childhood days.
Your small hand . . . how very long ago!

Oh you, small hand . . . so small in mine!
Oh, wind and light in your brown, silky hair!
Your childlike words . . . your laughing and your crying
Still rings in my ears, as if they had just occurred.

Even then in the enthusiasm of your play
There was a beautiful seriousness, my big, little man;
A foreshadowing of distant, but lofty goals
Spoke to me through your dark eyes.

At that point I knew: A God raises from those times
A life high enough to meet those standards.
We are only the stirrups of those who ride,
Whenever the dawn of a new age is revealed.

Go your way, my son in military frock.
That is a source of pride: You didn't turn back.
And when I hear in the blue, silky skies
The warlike buzz of iron birds,

Then your courage spurs me on to good day's deeds.
That I, my son, am of your blood,
That I bolster my heart through your heart,
Be, in all humility, my exquisite reward!

CHAPTER 1

"The Fate of Europe Is in Your Hands"

THE LIFE-AND-DEATH STRUGGLE OF THE GERMAN NATION AGAINST INTERNATIONAL BOLSHEVISM BEGINS

The road leading down to the Bug is lonely and quiet. The deep rumbling of the engines, which was present in the flood plain from evening until midnight, has turned silent. The prime movers have brought the guns and the antitank guns forward into position. The tanks are ready. Once again, everything is peaceful. The countryside appears to be asleep, as usual. Only the croaking of the massed choir of frogs ceaselessly continues its noise in the meadows.

We move past a motorcycle infantry company.[1] Another kilometer before we had to dismount. We continued along carefully under the concealment offered by the row of trees. Almost without noise, a German antitank gun was pushed forward. In a good hour, it would be a terrible wake-up call for the Bolsheviks on the far side of the Bug.

The firm path down the embankment only lasted a few more steps. The meadow pathway was soft and muddy. Your foot sank in deeply with every step. Wooden footpaths had been set up across ditches and small branches of the waterway.

---

1. Translator's Note: For operational security reasons, the actual unit and formation designations are not given. The motorcycle company in question would have belonged to *Kradschützen-Bataillon 3*. It is interesting to note that two different Manteuffels commanded the battalion, although neither was the most famous in the modern history of the officer family, Hasso-Eccard *Freiherr* von Manteuffel, who ended the war commanding a field army and being one of only 27 recipients of the Diamonds to the Oak Leaves and Swords to the Knight's Cross of the Iron Cross.

We reported to the commander and were briefed on the situation. The assembly area of our armored division, which was to force a crossing over the Bug, was to the south of Brest-Litovsk.

In a section of cultivated field in the middle of a pasture, foxholes had been dug. There were engineers squatting in them. The dark green waters of the Bug flashed through the pastures and alders. The river formed a serpentine course for 250 kilometers along the General Governorate of Poland and the Soviet Union, until it turned into the Vistula.

It was already fairly light. During the bright nights of June, it was barely dark even during moonless nights. Even around midnight, there was still a faint light in the skies.

The nights before an attack are always short. A natural tension and manly expectation pulsates through every soldier before the fight. This night is also one without sleep. We are positioned in a foxhole behind an old alder. The frog concert overpowers the whispering here and there. There was the slight clink of weapons. Carbines, machine guns, and ammunition cans are made ready. Engineers cut the wire of the obstacles along the river. There is a loud cracking sound in the stillness of the night. The assault boats are prepared. The thickly bulging tubes are pumped full.

They're all the same, these last days and hours before fateful campaigns and large battles. In every case, the soldier gets the feeling that things have come to a head. The general staff officers have finished their difficult preparatory work. They have thought everything through down to the last detail and stipulation. The generals have moved their command posts forward. In the woods and villages behind the front, the command pennants of the headquarters are the external sign that the field armies have finished their approach marches and that they have been directed to counterattack into a Bolshevist front that is prepared for offensive operations.[2] Then comes the day of decision—the famous H-Hour—the time that the attack has been ordered.

---

2. Translator's Note: The Germans long argued that the genesis of *Operation "Barbarossa"* was the plans and preparations Stalin was making for an attack on Germany. This line of argument was discounted after the war, but it was taken seriously in the mid-1980's with a book by a former Soviet intelligence officer, Victor Suvorov, *Icebreaker: Who Started the Second World War* (Viking Press/Hamish Hamilton: 1990), who argued essentially the same thing. This thesis is the subject of heated argument.

This time, the day of attack is Sunday, 21 June, at 0315 hours.[3] It's only thirty minutes until then. Half an hour before the start of the fateful struggle by Germany for life and death against Jewish Bolshevism. We think about our homeland, which can sleep peacefully in the protection of the ever-ready Eastern Front. We imagine what the faces of our loved ones at home will look like, when the call to arms of our *Führer* is read on the radio in the morning. During the campaign in the West, we only heard the exhortation in bits and pieces along the avenues of advance from those who had been fortunate enough to listen in on a radio set. Some didn't hear it until days later. This time, the historical words of the *Führer* and Supreme Commander were distributed to the forces in the field on flyers. When Hitler is allowed to break his silence, his first words are to the troops. His words accompany them into their attack and firing positions. That binds them all the more. Everyone perceives the greatness of the hour. There is no one who would not be gripped by it. It's understandable that they talk about it for a long time this night: "The fate of Europe, the future of the *Reich*, the existence of our people is now entirely in your hands."

The young soldiers cinch their helmet straps tighter. They know the responsibility that the *Führer* has placed on each of their shoulders. They lift their heads out of their positions and carefully peer across the river, quietly and with determination. Many questions circulate through our heads in these last minutes. Have the Bolshevists observed something from their observation towers? Is the far bank fortified? Are there bunkers over there? Will the friendly artillery hold down the enemy until the surprise attack has succeeded? Nothing can be seen over there. The banks of the rivers are overgrown, as is the case all over the east. High reeds, hedges, underbrush, and trees deny any type of insight.

Our glances drift ever more frequently to our watches. The large hand moves ever more quickly towards three. The tension reaches its high point. The last minute! The last minute before a campaign—the first tracers hiss towards the pale heavens. Then more guns join in, until a single, gigantic thunderclap rends the air. Antitank gunners send fiery tracers across the river. The reports of the artillery boom. A single aircraft

---

3. Translator's Note: German accounts generally use Central European Time, which was the official military time for the Germans and two hours earlier than the actual local time in the Soviet Union.

turns in small circles. It's the German aerial observer. Fires climb high on the other bank.

That colorful, fiery picture of the first few minutes sinks deeply and unforgettably into our consciousness. In the space of a pulse beat, we realize that the guns are growling from the North Polar Sea to the Black Sea. Then we run to the Bug.

THE DIVISIONAL HISTORY

The divisional history[4] records the events of this chapter as follows:

On 16 June 1941, the *3. Panzer-Division* moved into its assembly areas along the Bug. The advance parties of the battalions took off early in the morning. They had the mission of establishing quarters for the companies that followed and, if necessary, to assume the frontier security of the regiments of the *34. Infanterie-Division* deployed there. Towards evening, the lead elements of the *3. Panzer-Division* were along the Bug.

The *I./Schützen-Regiment 3* (*Major* Wellmann) moved into the area around Koden. The 2nd and 3rd Companies established noncommissioned officer posts up front along the river so as to be able to observe any movement across the river and to be on the alert for unusual noises or signals. The boundary with the friendly forces to the right—the *4. Panzer-Division*—ran from Olszanki as far as Point 151.8, four kilometers southeast of Stradecz.

The *II./Schützen-Regiment 394* (*Major Dr.* Müller[5]) was inserted to the left and was located in the area around Okszyn. Its observation posts were likewise located up front along the wire fence, which ran along the river. On the far side, the darkness of night spread itself out—the darkness of a foreign world. The friendly force to the left was the *45. Infanterie-Division*.

With those deployments, the *3. Panzer-Division* completed its occupation of the designated sector. The two rifle battalions were deployed along a narrow front up along the river; the rest of the division prepared for the upcoming mission in the rearward bivouac areas by conducting continuous route reconnaissance, small-scale exercises,

---

4. Translator's Note: Traditionsverband der 3. Panzer-Division, *Geschichte der 3. Panzer-Division* (Berlin: Verlag der Buchhandlung Günter Richter, 1967), 104–5.

5. Translator's Note: German convention is to list not only the military rank but also the academic degree in titles.

maintenance of its vehicles, and issuing basic loads of ammunition. On 16 June, *Generalleutnant* Model signed the operations plan for the attack of the *3. Panzer-Division* across the Bug on D-Day. Only the officers of the senior battle staff knew that D-Day was to be next Sunday.

CHAPTER 2

The First *Coup de Main*

CORPS ORDERS: "THROUGH AND FORWARD!"

"Through and forward!" — The commanding general of our armor corps[6] announced the orders of the *Führer* to his tankers with this proclamation. The officer who read the orders aloud to the assembled leaders of the formations turned off his flashlight. Ending with a hail to the *Führer*, the officers departed and went to their troop elements. Their motorcycles snaked their way along invisible paths to the tanks, which had been waiting, hidden, in the woods along the Bug for this order.

"Come over here! Have a drink! This is something worth having a drink for!" *Leutnant* M. put the bottle with the ginger liquor, which the commander of the engineers handed him, to his lips.[7] "It's advanced math, what I'm doing there. Doing this type of thing for the first time. Words fail me!"

The sound of steps approached the bridge. The *Oberst*[8] with the submachine gun.

---

6. Translator's Note: This was *General der Kavallerie* Leo Dietrich Franz *Reichsfreiherr* von Scheppenburg, the commanding general of the *XXIV. Armee-Korps (mot.)*. Schweppenburg was the commander of the *3. Panzer-Division* during the campaign in Poland. On 9 July 1944, he received the Knight's Cross to the Iron Cross for the performance of his corps during the summer fighting. He went on to command two other corps by war's end. Following the war, he was instrumental in helping form the new *Bundeswehr*. He died in 1974.

7. Translator's Note: In the interest of operational security, none of the individuals are named. *Panzer-Pionier-Bataillon 39* was the divisional engineer battalion and was lead by *Major* Beigel at the time. He commanded the battalion through 27 September 1941, when he was succeeded by *Major* Heinz Petsch. Beigel was awarded the Knight's Cross to the Iron Cross on 9 July 1941 and ended the war as an *Oberst*.

8. Translator's Note: Based on the descriptions and information provided in this chapter, the *Oberst* in question is probably Kleemann, the commander of *Schützen-Regiment 3* and leader of *Gruppe Oberst Kleeman*. Likewise, the engineers in question are probably from the assault detachment of the *3./Pionier-Bataillon 39*, which was a part of the *Kampfgruppe*.

"Well, is it going to work?"

"It most certainly will, *Herr Oberst!*"

A few directives were issued: Suspicious buildings on the far bank—a white spot here, a different field position apparently over there. Everything was in their heads. Covering fire would be provided by heavy machine guns. An antitank gun had been set up and was ready to move, its crew hunched behind it.

It slowly turned light. We went forward as far as the barbed wire, which formed the frontier. One touch and it would fall. It had been slightly undermined the previous night. Our guys were already to the left of the bridge on the island in the river. Floats were already along the banks. The *Leutnant* made a slight shift to the right and looked across the river with his binoculars. That was the signal that had been agreed upon. At the same moment, the swimmers pushed off from the banks, working their way towards the bridge in order to remove any demolitions that might be there. The *Leutnant* took off with a sudden jolt and raced across the bridge, followed by two men. There were figures on the far side. Slight pressure on the trigger—they disappeared into the grass. We raced behind him, together with the riflemen and the motorcycles, which immediately pressed forward. Hands on the bundled charge; a look at the spot where the road started on the far side. Was the bridge going to go up? Was it not going to go up? Well? Now? At least if it went up at that point, we were already across!

The impacts in front of us—barely noticed—were the artillery preparation. It was being fired with the precision of a clock. The companies along the banks fired with tracers. We soon fired white signal flares; otherwise, they would be engaging us shortly. They couldn't have any idea how far we already were. Six men with shovels were filling in the broad channel right on the other side of the bridge. An antitank gun was already in front of it. The gun wanted to cross, but it was unable to. It went around and slid down the embankment to the right, along with its crew. Anxious moments. We pulled and pulled, but it did not want to become dislodged. Give it some more effort! Fifteen men were involved at that point, giving it the heave-ho. Then it shot out of the ditch. Was there still no fire? Were the Bolsheviks still sleeping? Have they scrammed? It really didn't matter. The main thing was that we had the bridge. Looking back, we could see the tanks approaching the German side of the bank.

Lightning bolts of fire arched across the river. The brilliant red light of a gigantic fire was already rising above the woods in the distance. The city was burning! Banks of fog drew across the skies. The first rays of the sun felt their way above them. The impacts of our artillery blazed in the woods ahead of us.

The *Oberst* on the bridge spurred the engineers on. The way was cleared immediately. The *Oberst* could immediately issue the order to form up to march. The heavy tanks started rumbling their way towards us. A hair's breadth away along the railings, they pressed passed the engineers still working on the bridge. The bridge groaned. The tank commanders looked out of their cupolas.

"Is it really intact? That's great how everything worked out once again!"

The reconnaissance aircraft were already flapping their way above us to the east, departing with a curve. They saw the white signal flares coming out of the woods ahead of us, they saw our boats on the river, and they saw the tanks on our intact bridge.

The attack of the armor corps was rolling.

THE DIVISIONAL HISTORY

The divisional history[9] records the events of this chapter as follows:

The *3. Berlin-Brandenburgische Panzer-Division* was attached to *Panzergruppe 2* (*Generaloberst* Guderian) for employment in Russia. The *Panzergruppe* was part of the *4. Armee* of *Heeresgruppe Mitte*. For the initial part of the operation, the *Panzergruppe* had received the mission of crossing the Bug on both sides of Brest-Litowsk and reaching the area bounded by Roslawl–Jelnja–Smolensk. From there, it was to turn in the direction of either Moscow or Leningrad, in conjunction with *Panzergruppe 3*.

The *XXIV. Armee-Korps (mot)* marched over the course of the next few days with the *255. Infanterie-Division* in the area around Wlodawa, with the intent of marching on Maloryta from there. The *1. Kavallerie-Division* adjoined it and was to turn in the direction of Pinsk from Slawatycze later on. The *3. Panzer-Division* and *4. Panzer-Division* had the mission of breaking out of the area around Koden and reaching the Brest–Kobryn road. The *10. Infanterie-Division (mot)* remained behind the armored divisions as the reserve.

---

9. Translator's Note: Traditionsverband, *Geschichte*, 106.

The *3. Panzer-Division* organized itself for *Unternehmen "Barbarossa"* into the following *Kampfgruppen*[10]:

• Headquarters, *3. Panzer-Division* (*Generalleutnant* Model with *Major i.G.*[11] Pomtow as the division operations officer) with *Nachrichten-Abteilung 39, Straßenbau-Bataillon 97*,[12] and the *9.(H)/Lehr Geschwader 2*[13] at Katy.

• *Gruppe Oberstleutnant Audörsch*, consisting of *Schützen-Regiment 394, SS-Pionier-Bataillon "Das Reich"* (only for the crossing),[14] the *2./Pionier-Bataillon 39*, the *1./Panzerjäger-Abteilung 543*,[15] the engineer platoon of *Kradschützen-Bataillon 3* and the *1. Radfahr-Bau-Bataillon 503*.[16] These formations and elements were located in the northern portion of the division sector, between Kopytow and the Bug.

• *Gruppe Oberst Kleemann* assembled in the south in the area around Koden. Belonging to *Oberst* Kleemann's forces were *Schützen-Regiment 3, Pionier-Bataillon 10*,[17] the *1./Pionier-Bataillon 39*, the *2.* and *3./Panzerjäger-Abteilung 543*, the headquarters and *2./Radfahr-Bau-Bataillon 503*, a reinforced company from the *III./Panzer-Regiment 6, Brücko 606* with the *2./403*,[18] and an assault detachment from the *3./Pionier-Bataillon 39*.

---

10. Translator's Note: *Kampfgruppe* can be translated as "battle group," but it can be as small as a company-size entity (a company team in U.S. Army usage) or a battalion-size force (a task force in U.S. Army usage). It is an *ad hoc* formation, usually consisting of combined arms with a predominantly armored, infantry, or reconnaissance force base. In accordance with standard German practice, it was named after its commander.
11. Translator's Note: *i.G.* = *im Generalstab* = General Staff officer. Generally, General Staff Officers were assigned to divisions as the operations and logistics officers. They continued to wear the carmine-colored branch color on their insignia facings and added the suffix *i.G.* after their rank to denote their status.
12. Translator's Note: 97th Engineer Battalion (Road Construction).
13. Translator's Note: 9th Section (Army)/2nd Instructional Wing. Each armored division had an aerial liaison/observation section assigned to it. They generally flew the light utility aircraft, the Fieseler *Storch* (Stork).
14. Translator's Note: This was the engineer battalion of *SS-Division "Reich,"* a formation of what was to become known as the *Waffen-SS* (Armed *SS*). The official designation of the battalion was *Pionier-Bataillon SS-Division Reich*.
15. Translator's Note: 543rd Antitank Battalion, a corps asset.
16. Translator's Note: 1st Company of the 503rd Engineer Battalion (Bicycle), another corps asset. This formation used bicycles as its means of transport.
17. Translator's Note: The 10th Engineer Battalion was the combat engineer battalion of the *10. Infanterie-Division (mot)*, which was being held back as the corps ready reserve. For a forced river-crossing operation, the engineer battalions of the forces not immediately committed to the forced crossing are usually attached in direct support of the lead forces.
18. Translator Note: These are corps bridging assets.

- *Gruppe Oberst Linnarz* was located around Zcuprov with *Panzer-Regiment 6, Panzerjäger-Abteilung 521,* leichte *Flak-Abteilung 91,*[19] one heavy battery of the *I./Flak-Regiment 11,*[20] and the *3./Pionier-Bataillon 39.* It followed the division.

- *Gruppe Major von Corvin-Wierbitzki* with *Kradschützen-Bataillon 3, Aufklärungs-Abteilung 1* and the *6./Flak-Abteilung 59.* This *Kampfgruppe* was located in the Katy and Zcuprov area.

---

19. Translator's Note: This was a *Luftwaffe* formation. It was originally an antiaircraft battalion in the Austrian military before its assimilation into the *Wehrmacht* after the *Anschluß* in 1938.
20. Translator's Note: *Flak-Regiment 11* was also a *Luftwaffe* antiaircraft formation in direct support of the division.

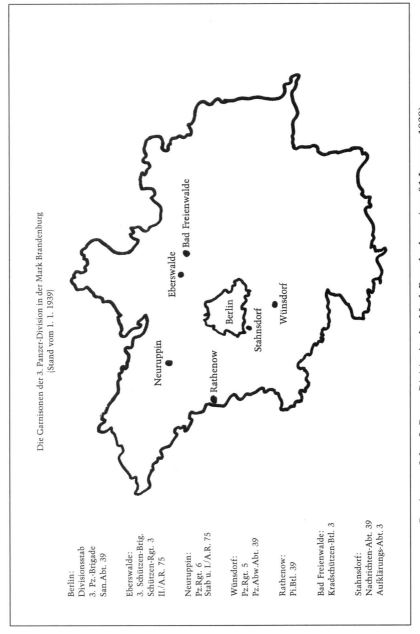

Die Garnisonen der 3. Panzer-Division in der Mark Brandenburg
(Stand vom 1. 1. 1939)

Berlin:
Divisionsstab
3. Pz.-Brigade
San.Abt. 39

Eberswalde:
3. Schützen-Brig.
Schützen-Rgt. 3
II./A.R. 75

Neuruppin:
Pz.Rgt. 6
Stab u. I./A.R. 75

Wünsdorf:
Pz.Rgt. 5
Pz.Abw.Abt. 39

Rathenow:
Pi.Btl. 39

Bad Freienwalde:
Kradschützen-Btl. 3

Stahnsdorf:
Nachrichten-Abt. 39
Aufklärungs-Abt. 3

Garrisons of the *3. Panzer-Division* in the Mark Brandenburg (as of 1 January 1939).

The division coat of arms—a rampant bear, indicative of its headquarters in Berlin—as well as two of the vehicular tactical symbols employed by the division.

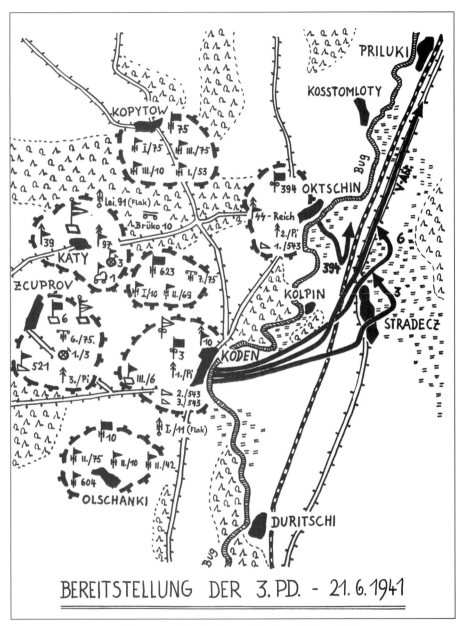

BEREITSTELLUNG DER 3. PD. - 21. 6. 1941

Assembly area of the *3. Panzer-Division* (21 June 1941).

The *Führer* during a situation briefing in the main headquarters.

Generaloberst Guderian, commander in chief of an armored field army in the East and recipient of the Knight's Cross to the Iron Cross with Oak Leaves. The field army he commanded was initially *Panzergruppe 2* (*Panzergruppe Guderian*) and was redesignated as the *2. Panzer-Armee* in October 1941.

General der Panzertruppen Freiherr von Schweppenburg, commanding general of an armored corps in the East and recipient of the Knight's Cross to the Iron Cross. At the time of this book, von Schweppenburg commanded the *XXIV. Armee-Korps (mot.)*. He was also the first commander of the division, albeit for a short time (1 September 1939 to 7 October 1939).

Generaloberst Model, our division commander in the East until assuming command of an armored corps. He received the Knight's Cross to the Iron Cross with Oak Leaves. Model was the commander of the division for most of the period referenced in this book. He became the commanding general of the *XXXXI. Panzer-Korps* when he left the division. Note that the Knight's Cross was added to the photograph, a common practice when current photographs with the latest awards were not available.

Generalmajor Breith, our current division commander and recipient of the Knight's Cross to the Iron Cross with Oak Leaves. Breith commanded the division for exactly one year, before ultimately assuming command of the *III. Panzer-Korps*, a position he held until the end of the war.

0315 hours, 22 June 1941: *Coup de main* against the bridge over the Bug at Koden. Combat engineers put finishing touches on a seven-ton temporary bridge over impassable terrain.

The heavy weapons are transported across with pneumatic boats. In this instance, the weapon is a 3.7cm antitank gun. The crates on the gun shield are ammunition boxes for the single-piece rounds. The 3.7cm antitank gun was the German Army's standard antitank weapon at the start of the war and through the start of Operation Barbarossa. It was adequate against the initial armor encountered by the Germans, primarily light tanks such as the BT-5, but was hopelessly inadequate when the T-34 and the KV-series of tanks arrived at the front. At that point, it was derisively referred to as the army's "door knocker," since the only thing it appeared able to do was announce its presence to the enemy.

In the direction of hard fighting. Elements of a motorcycle battalion move forward past supply vehicles. Of interest are the railway tracks that parallel the road. They appear to be of narrow gauge. One of the problems the Germans encountered during their invasion was the fact that the standard Russian railway line was wider than European ones, necessitating the conversion of the lines as the German forces advanced in order to receive logistical support by rail. This not only affected supply—a chronic problem of German forces in the field—but it also deflected manpower and other assets as long as the lines had to be converted and, once partisan warfare began in earnest, defended.

Our combat engineers remove a tree obstacle. This obstacle was probably only a "hasty" one, inasmuch as a true *abatis* requires the felling of trees on both sides of a roadway to ensure intermeshing of the fallen vegetation, making it more difficult to negotiate and remove.

Our armor deploys for an attack: A classic view of maneuver warfare. Seen here are both tanks and armored personnel carriers deployed in battle formation . . .

. . . and they are already behind Sluzk. An artillery version of the light armored personnel carrier, the *Sd.Kfz. 253*, is in the foreground, while the standard array of German armor—minus the already obsolescent *Panzer I* and the Skoda *Panzer 35(t)* and *38(t)*—are seen in the background: the *Panzer II*, the *Panzer III*, and the *Panzer IV*. Note that the artillery vehicle has a covered superstructure. It is also carrying a bundle of fascines on its front grill, to be used in assisting in the negotiation of small obstacles and muddy terrain.

A hot day: Artillery supports the advance of the division. The *schwere Feldhaubitze 18* (*sFH 18*) was the standard heavy artillery piece (15cm) of divisional artillery. It was usually only issued to one battalion, which had three batteries of six guns each.

Heavy artillery in action. It was the artillery that caused the greatest casualties, not small-arms fire. Surprisingly, the one gunner does not wear any protection for his hands for tossing aside the hot spent casings.

On dusty roads through the woods of White Ruthenia. This prime mover and *leichtes Infanterie-Geschütz 18* (7.5cm) was usually found in the heavy-weapons companies of divisional infantry regiments. It was designed to provide the regimental commander with immediate direct-fire support for his forces. In this image, it appears that some infantry have hitched a ride with the gun crew.

The seemingly endless steppes. Infantry march across the vast open spaces of the Soviet Union. The lead soldier with the *MP40* is an officer and probably a platoon leader or the company commander. Despite the laurels the armored divisions received, it was the infantry divisions that were often given the mission of clearing and holding the terrain that the fast-moving mechanized divisions were unable to secure.

The *Sd.Kfz. 251* with externally mounted racks for launching 28cm or 32cm rockets. The ground *Stuka*, as it was referred to by the common German soldier, was not terribly accurate, but it could blanket a large area with high-explosive rounds in a short period and had a tremendously demoralizing effort among defending enemy soldiers. There were normally several of these in each armored division's combat engineer battalion.

Headquarters and staff vehicles from the *11. Panzer-Division* pass a knocked-out Soviet armored car, a BA 10, which was armed with 4.5-centimeter main gun, far heavier than anything used by comparable German reconnaissance vehicles of the time.

CHAPTER 3

150 Kilometers in a Single Day!

DEEP THRUST INTO THE ENEMY

When the commander of our armored division issued orders to continue the advance on the second day of the war, each of the men had the feeling that much would be achieved and wrested from the enemy on this day. The division moved out in the early morning hours at a river crossing. During their hurried flight the previous evening, the Soviets had succeeded in setting the bridge on fire and the combat engineers had been able to get it ready again in uninterrupted nighttime work. At the same time, a sixteen-ton bridge was erected at another point on the river. The advance guard of the armored division was the first formation to cross there. Its mission was to grab hold of the enemy again, drive him along, and, wherever he attempted to establish a defense, eliminate him.

Nothing happened during the first ten kilometers, but the tank company, which was the point element of the advance guard, caught up with the rearguard of the enemy formations and immediately went into action. The first enemy tanks were knocked out, enemy pockets of resistance neutralized, and enemy artillery pieces captured. Above all, the enemy's retreat was transformed into hurried flight by the hard pressing of our forces. The intermediate objective of the division was the city of Kobrin. There was an important bridge over the Muchawiez that needed to be taken and secured. The enemy had established himself in the villages, woods, and houses outside the city, but he was overrun by the combined efforts of the tanks, the motorcycle infantry, the antitank elements, and the engineers. The Bolsheviks had transformed the houses in the city into pockets of resistance and employed armored vehicles for the street fighting. But none of that helped him. In a short fifteen minutes, the houses from which fire was coming were burning and the enemy tanks were ablaze in the streets. A platoon of motorcycle infantry and tanks immediately seized the bridge. Although the city still had to be cleared of scattered enemy elements and snipers, the advance of the point guard continued apace so as to reach the new march objective.

The events that happened along that 50-to-60-kilometer stretch of road between Kobrin and Bereza-Kartuska serve as a great example of the striking power and momentum of our armored forces, as they plowed their way through the enemy. One can only compare the fighting of the advance guard with the steel-hard edge of a wedge, which is driven into the enemy with irresistible power and which breaks all resistance. To cover its flight, the enemy had employed guns of all calibers—up to 21-centimeter howitzers—light and heavy tanks, antitank guns, and infantry formations. But all resistance was in vain against the force of the German armored breakthrough. Although the Bolsheviks fired with everything they had from their rifles, tanks and guns, the German cannons and machine guns were always faster. They hammered into the enemy with an unimaginable quickness and precision. The enemy was completely overwhelmed and forced into hasty flight, leaving behind a large number of armored vehicles and guns, many of which were destroyed. The degree of haste could be seen in the innumerable burning or crew-abandoned armored vehicles and guns. Just along that fifty-kilometer avenue of advance alone, there were sixty Soviet tanks and an equal number of light and heavy guns that were captured or destroyed.

Since the enemy realized the futility of organized resistance, he adopted new methods. The Bolsheviks fled from the roads and into the woods and marshlands and conducted a war of ambush against the German formations that were continuing to advance. As a result, the motorcycle infantry had to dismount almost every fifteen minutes to clear patches of woods, marshland and villages of Soviet forces. The motorcycle infantry and the tanks constantly advanced and passed one another. Leapfrogging, they overran every resistance of the enemy and were actually able to reach the day's objective by the afternoon. Once there, they immediately established a ten-kilometer-deep bridgehead.

Our armored division had driven a wedge almost 100 kilometers into the enemy on this one day and had reached a day's objective that had seemed quite bold early that morning.

But that was not the end of things. Immediately after Bereza-Kartuska was taken, the division commander summoned the leaders of his elements together and issued new orders to continue the advance that same evening and take the river crossing fifty kilometers away that was of extreme importance for the continued advance. Towards 1900 hours, a reorganized advance guard moved out. That initiated an advance that was led in such an unbelievably bold and fantastic manner that none of the men who participated could ever forget it. The tanks and the motorcycle infantry advanced into the twilight. The Bolsheviks had hunkered down in every woodline and every village, since they had assumed that the Germans would be happy with the capture of Bereza-Kartuska and not continue their advance until the following morning. Despite that, heavy fires greeted our forward units from the woods and the villages. It ricocheted harmlessly off of the tanks, however, and they immediately transitioned to the attack, shooting the villages and armored vehicles, to pieces. The armored advance was soon marked for kilometers by burning woods, armored vehicles and villages. The advance guard continued to attack, frequently moving past exploding ammunition vehicles, past burning villages, which were a sea of flames, and through woods, from which the Bolsheviks constantly fired at us with machine guns and rifles. That was no obstacle for the tanks, but even the motorcycle infantry and riflemen silenced the fires of the snipers by blazing away into the woods and the villages from their combat vehicles and motorcycles with everything they had. The first bridge was soon reached, then the second, third, and fourth. By then, it was clear to everyone why the division commander had ordered the continued advance and attack. If the Bolsheviks had succeeded in destroying these many bridges and, above all, the major crossing point, then our advance could have been held up for days, since that route was the only possible road for our advance. In that area, which stretched for many hundreds of kilometers, there was nothing next to the road on either the right or the left except ponds, marshland, and jungle-like woods.

A railway crossing and a nearby freight yard where the Bolsheviks had fortified themselves had to be taken. The freight yard was immediately covered with fire from all of the main guns and rifles, and it was set ablaze in short order. After advancing for two hours, the advance guard had closed to within three kilometers of the bridge. The high point of the day's fighting was about to come. All of a sudden, artillery and machine-gun fire was placed on and along the avenue of advance; it was a fire that covered the road precisely and accurately. But the desire to attack could not be crippled so close to the objective. A motorcycle infantry and a tank company employed against the bridge were actually able to put it in our hands, complete and undamaged. While the motorcycle infantry covered the bridge, the tanks advanced another ten kilometers in order to eliminate a battery that was covering the approach route. The German tanks advanced in complete darkness and fired at anything that showed itself with their main guns and machine guns. They silenced the battery and armored vehicles and then suddenly encountered an artillery battalion that was in the process of retreating. Completely surprised, the battalion was unable to defend itself. It was ruthlessly overrun in an attack and eliminated.

In a day of uninterrupted fighting, our armored division had boxed its way approximately 150 kilometers deep into the enemy. In the process, it captured or destroyed 107 enemy tanks, more than 100 guns of all calibers, ammunition vehicles, and extensive amounts of materiel in terms of equipment and ammunition, which the Bolsheviks had to leave behind in their flight. Most importantly, in the end, it had also wrested the river flood plain from the enemy. A day had come to a close that would probably remain without equal in the history of our armored formations and which bears honorable testimony to the offensive spirit and will to victory of our division.

THE HISTORY OF *PANZER-REGIMENT 6*

The regimental history of *Panzer-Regiment 6* records the events of this chapter as follows:[1]

Hauptmann Schneider-Kostalski[2] could not allow his men any rest. Together with the reconnaissance battalion, he advanced another sixty-five kilometers farther east and reached the regional capital of Bereza-Kartuska at 1900 hours. During that wild advance, numerous Russian columns fleeing to the east were shot up or swept aside. The Russians fled into the thick woods or the nearby grain fields and took the troops that followed under fire from there. They frequently had to dismount and smoke out the enemy from his hiding places in close combat. Polish farmers alerted the forces to the enemy positions. Because of that, the light platoon of the regiment (*Leutnant* Jakobs), which was reconnoitering along the right flank, was able to surprise six heavy guns being towed by tractors near Podberje and take the crews prisoner.

---

1. Translator's Note: Oskar Munzel, *Gekämpft, gesiegt, verloren* (Herford and Bonn: E.S. Mittler und Söhne, 1980), 68.
2. Translator's Note: Schneider-Kostalski was the acting commander of the 3rd Battalion. He received the Knight's Cross to the Iron Cross on 9 July 1941.

THE DIVISIONAL HISTORY

The divisional history[3] records the events of this chapter as follows:

Panzer-Regiment 6 was awakened at 0430 hours, since the trains had arrived with the valuable fuel. Immediately after refueling, the tanks rumbled off. The *III./Panzer-Regiment 6* took the lead. The advance proceeded terribly slowly. The road was very sandy, and the combat vehicles could only churn through slowly. Despite that, the lighter vehicles of the advance guard moved forward and were soon outside of Kobryn, which the Russians were defending.

Shortly after 1100 hours, the *III./Panzer-Regiment 6* arrived. Jabbing hard, the enemy pockets of resistance on the western side of the locality were eliminated. When entering the city, Russian light tanks appeared, all of which were shot to pieces. Likewise, high-explosive rounds crashed into the houses from which Russian machine-gun fire had flared up. After a quarter of an hour, the battalion had quashed all resistance.

The motorcycle infantry had advanced into the city center and were able to take the bridge over the Bug-Dnjepr Canal through rapid action. Unfortunately, the battalion suffered its first total losses in vehicles. Killed on this day were four noncommissioned officers and one *Obergefreiter* of the 12th Company and the Headquarters Company of the 3rd Battalion.

The regiment moved through the city quickly and reached the roads leading east with all of its elements. Up front were the lead elements of *Aufklärungs-Abteilung 1 (Hauptmann* Ziervogel) and *Kradschützen-Bataillon 3* (*Major* von Corvin-Wiersbitzki). That was the start of a journey that would be characteristic of this 23 June 1941.

Those vehicles of the *3. Panzer-Division* ceaselessly advanced along the broad road. There was no way to detour, since untrafficable moorland stretched to the right and left of the road. The Russians had been driven from the road. It was only the vehicles, guns, tossed-away weapons, and abandoned equipment that reminded one that the enemy had pulled back in flight. Our tanks occasionally had difficulty in maneuvering past the enemy vehicles, which were often perpendicular to the road. The Soviet riflemen had fled into the tall cornfields and fired from there on the following German columns in their open cross-country vehicles. The forces had to dismount and expel the Russians with cold steel.

The *I./Panzer-Regiment 6* made surprise contact with Russian tanks at 1540 hours at Buchowiecze. The enemy combat vehicles had broken out

---

3. Translator's Note: Traditionsverband, *Geschichte*, 110–12.

of nearby woods and taken the German columns under fire. *Major* Schmid-Ott[4] immediately employed his companies in an enveloping maneuver and knocked out thirty-six T-26's in the counterthrust. In the process, the *2./ Panzer-Regiment 6* (*Oberleutnant* Buchterkirch)[5] was able to finish off twelve tanks all by itself within the space of a few minutes. Polish peasants alerted the German tank crews passing by of hidden Russian defensive positions. The light platoon of *Panzer-Regiment 6* (*Leutnant* Jacobs) was directed towards the small village of Podberje off of the avenue of advance. The combat vehicles encountered six heavy guns and tractors there. The Russian cannoneers were so surprised by the appearance of German tanks that they surrendered. The *7./Panzer-Regiment 6*, which had been reinforced with medium tanks, was ordered forward to the 3rd Battalion to support it in its various skirmishes with fleeing Soviet columns.

The advance guard reached the regional capital of Bereza-Kartuska on the railway line to Minsk. It was able to break the initial resistance with its own forces, before *Panzer-Regiment 6* closed up. German prisoners—they came from the *4. Panzer-Division*—were freed from the hands of the Russians there. The advance guard and the tank regiment were far to the front. The rifle brigade could only follow slowly, since the solitary road was jammed. As lead regiment, *Schützen-Regiment 394* encountered no resistance. The intensity of the fighting by the divisional elements to the front could be gauged by the wrecks of enemy vehicles along the edge of the road, however.

The division command post was moved through Zabinka to Kobryn that day. The battle staff established itself in a church east of the bridge. The local populace was overwhelmingly friendly to the Germans and fed the rearward trains and supplies elements. Valuable material concerning the Soviet 4th Army fell into the hands of the intelligence officer; the

---

4. Translator's Note: Gustav Albrecht Schmidt-Ott was one of the first recipients of the newly created German Cross in Gold on 18 October 1941. He went on to receive the Knight's Cross of the Iron Cross on 3 October 1942 as an *Oberstleutnant* and acting commander of the regiment. Although Traditionsverband, *Geschichte,* spells his name as Schmid, most accounts give it as Schmidt.

5. Translator's Note: Ernst-Georg Buchterkirch was already a recipient of the Knight's Cross at the time of this action, having been awarded it on 26 June 1940 as a platoon leader in the 2nd Company for the fighting in France. He went on to receive the Oak Leaves to the Knight's Cross to the Iron Cross on 31 December 1943. At the time, he was still an *Oberleutnant,* but he was the company commander of the 2nd Company. He was the 44th recipient of this level of the award.

headquarters of the field army had been in Kobryn. That field army, under the command of Major General Korobkow, opposed *Panzergruppe 2* with its four rifle divisions, the 6th, the 42nd, the 49th, and the 75th. The XIV Corps (Mechanized) of Major General Oborin formed the second line of defense in the Pruzana–Kobryn area; its lines had been broken through by the *3. Panzer-Division* on 23 June.

Despite the success, *Generalleutnant* Model didn't allow his soldiers any rest. He personally went to Bereza-Kartuska and ordered the ceaseless pursuit of the fleeing enemy. *Major* Beigel, the commander of *Pionier-Bataillon 39*, quickly reorganized the advance guard and immediately continued the advance. The combat vehicles and motorcycles advanced without regard to the withdrawing enemy elements along the road. Villages and woods were negotiated, bridges over the many small waterways were crossed, and the resistance that flared up along the flanks was swiftly engaged. The Russian defenses along the railway crossing southwest of Byrten were stronger. The light armored cars fired with everything they had. The wooden freight terminal soon went up in flames. The first tanks arrived soon thereafter.

All of a sudden, well-aimed artillery fire was placed on the road. There was no getting around it, however. The tanks, followed by the motorcycles, rattled on. The forces moved three kilometers farther into the night—through woods and Soviet artillery fire. The lead platoon of the *7./Panzer-Regiment 6* (*Leutnant* Rühl) was in front of the bridge at the first crossing over the Szczara at 2200 hours. The tanks rolled across the wooden bridge without incident. They then advanced a few more kilometers. The motorcycle infantry and the engineers secured the small bridgehead. The tanks then returned in the darkness and rested.

On that second day of the war, the *3. Panzer-Division* had broken through the enemy front and advanced 150 kilometers, destroying 107 Russian combat vehicles. Several hundred artillery pieces of all calibers were captured or destroyed. The leader of the advance guard, *Major* Beigel, became the first officer of the *3. Panzer-Division* to receive the Knight's Cross in the East. The official recommendation read, in part: "By means of lightning-fast action, [he] took the important bridge over the Szczara, which created the prerequisite for the rapid advance of an armored corps."

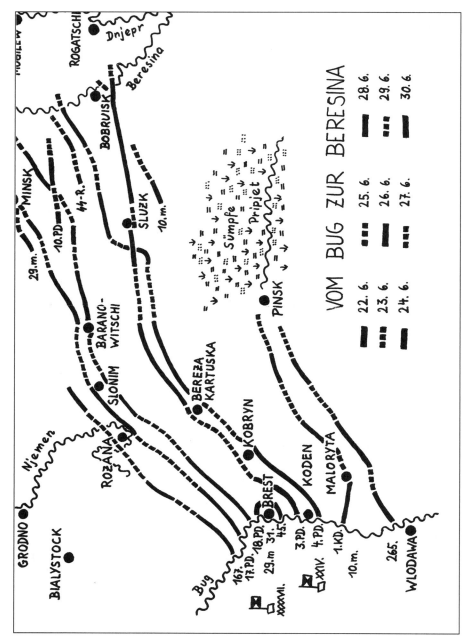

From the Bug to the Beresina.
(Sümpfe Pripjet = Pripet Marshes)

CHAPTER 4

The Beresina Is Reached

UNIQUELY VICTORIOUS MARCH IN ONE WEEK TO THE HISTORIC RIVER

We were at the outer wall of the citadel of Brobruisk. The forward-observer positions of the artillery were located there. The earth was wet. There was water in the foxholes. After hot days, there had been a storm yesterday with a cloudburst. It continued to pour buckets this day was well. The clouds hung low. The silvery ribbon of the famous Beresina flowed quietly and lazily in front of us. It had been a fateful river to Napoleon's army. Banks of fog wafted over the blooming meadows. The steel bridge along the main road had been blown up. Yesterday, the fortress walls had trembled from impacting heavy artillery. The Soviet artillery was holding the city and the citadel under fire. Bomber squadrons of the Reds dropped a hail of iron upon us. In the evening, the commander of the howitzer battery was killed. It was almost quiet up front this day. There was only the individual barking of machine-gun fire. German patrols were on the other side of the Beresina.

It was Sunday. A week had passed since we had gone over the Bug last Sunday. The rapid advance was held up for hours. The engineers first had to construct a new bridge. We moved back into the city. In one of the wooden houses abandoned by its inhabitants, we attempted to organize and write down the innumerable impressions and images that had impressed themselves upon all of us with the force of a flood.

A natural bulwark was present in front of the Soviet Republic and Moscow, its heart. It is White Ruthenia.[1] As a result of a terror campaign, it is one of sixteen federal republics, a region distinctly marked by woods and marsh—one of the most formidable obstacles for operations and movements of large formations. Between Grodno and Brest-Litowsk, its new

---

1. Translator's Note: This roughly corresponds to the eastern portion of present-day Belarus.

borders stuck its pointed nose deeply towards East Prussia and the General Governorate. In its south, in the direction of the Ukraine, the infamous Pripet (Rokitno) Marsh spreads out. In an area 200 kilometers wide, there is a barely passable belt that runs nearly 500 kilometers from west to east. There are only a few trails here, which are known only to the locals. This wooded marshland around the Polessje, which can only be negotiated in a dry summer by infantry in open order, is a good flank guard for an attacking field army.

By nature, White Ruthenia has been marked as a transitory route between Berlin and Moscow. In the course of a long history, armies marched in both directions. Of importance—decisively so—is the possession of the few improved roads and transportation hubs. They dominate the land. It was for that reason that the wedges of armor advanced there. Point of departure: Brest-Litowsk. The old fortress is also an important constellation of roads at the gates to White Ruthenia, which, with its 228,000 square kilometers, is almost as large as the former Yugoslavia.

Two main routes lead north of the Pripet across the Dnjepr and into the Soviet Union. One leads through Minsk, the capital of White Ruthenia. From there, it runs as a so-called *Autobahn* through Smolensk, the entry point to the greater Russian area. It has a surface running from twelve to fifteen meters across. It is the best road in Soviet Russia. To the south, like the second track of a railway, is the main road leading through Kobrin and Sluzk to Bobruisk on the Beresina. The Soviet capital is also located at its end. Those two roads have temporarily become the "routes"[2] for our armored group.

The sun was already burning hot in the morning along the broad, firm-packed gravel main road of White Ruthenia. It was Tuesday, the third day of the campaign. Covered in a veil of dust, the long columns rolled and rattled again. We were moving along the tank road that goes through Sluzk and Rogatschew (on the Dnjepr) and lead to Moscow, exactly 1,040

2. Translator's Note: The original German uses *Rollbahn*, which has several meanings, usually avenue of advance (or withdrawal) or supply route. Since the term is used ironically here, given the poor condition and paucity of Soviet roadways, it has been translated as "route."

kilometers away. The lead elements of the armored corps were already far
out to the front. They were fighting along the Schtschara, a tributary of
the Memel, 200 kilometers from Brest-Litowsk. That was already beyond
Baranowitschi to the north.

On that day, the area around the citadel of the old fortress of Brest-
Litowsk was wrested from the enemy. An infantry division, Austrians from
the homeland of the *Führer*, had assaulted the city and its outer works in
a lightning-fast operation. The citadel still had not been taken, however.
Thousands of Bolsheviks were encircled. They defended with a desperate
wildness. But it was only a matter of hours before their resistance would
be broken. Of decisive importance for the large-scale operations was that
the bridges fell into our hands intact. While German artillery hammered
against the walls, casemates, and military facilities, machine-guns rattled
and hand grenades burst; our armored divisions were already storming
deep into White Ruthenia.

Of importance to our armor corps was the bridge at the small frontier
locality of Koden, to the south of the fortress. It was one of the few
crossing points over the Bug that had not been destroyed. A bold *coup
de main* succeeded. The first tanks immediately rattled across towards the
avenue of advance. Ever since then, the chain comprised of the field-gray
armyworm has never been rent asunder. The image that we had become
familiar with but which never ceased to fill us with enthusiasm—the
marching of the mechanized forces—repeated itself.

On the far side of the transportation hub of Kobrin, a former Polish
garrison, was a shot-up Soviet tank in the middle of the road. Blue smoke
continued to pour out of its hatches and holes. Dead Soviet soldiers were
in the roadside ditch. A long train of prisoners marched past, apathetic.
From that point forward, the road was literally lined with tanks and guns
of all calibers. An impressive and eloquent path of destruction. For us, it
was a new route of victory. The harsh signs of war demonstrated the force
and boldness with which the *Panzerwaffe* had struck again. It had overrun
the enemy in its first attack.

The German main guns are a proud and hard weapon. Working
together with the *Stukas*, they evoke horror and fear in the enemy. Large
bomb craters, placed precisely next to the road, showed their destructive
power once beyond Kobrin. The military facilities had been badly
battered—carbonized tree stumps and ripped-apart gun positions in a

cratered landscape. There, eight kilometers behind the city, enemy tanks suddenly appeared in the flanks. German destroyer aircraft identified them and chased them with their ten-kilogram bombs. They were driven right in front of a marching tank battalion. The companies did a "left face" on the road and fired as if on a gunnery range; thirty-six tanks of the T-26 variety with a 4.5-centimeter main gun—the pride of Moscow—remained where they were.

The Bolsheviks attempted to save their heavy artillery at the last minute. They did not succeed. The tanks were faster than the horses and the ungainly tractors. The German aviators chased the cannoneers and drivers into the woods. In a panic, they frequently jumped off their prime movers while they were still moving. The prime movers kept going until they turned over in a ditch. The guns, up to 21 centimeters, were spotted at regular intervals. Occasionally, they almost blocked the avenue of advance, two or three abreast. All modern guns. They never fired a shot. In most cases, their breechblocks still had the protective covers. Scattered everywhere were numerous machine guns: the water-cooled Maxim machine gun of two wheels—famous from the World War—as well as a couple of quad machine guns intended for antiaircraft duty.

The road to Bereza-Kartuska runs straight as an arrow, as if drawn by a ruler. There are also large military facilities there from Polish times as well. As a result, the city had to be bombed. A portion of its houses is destroyed. In the military facilities to the right of the road, the armored corps set up its command post for a short period. In the parade area are primitive posters that glorify the offensive spirit of the Soviet Army. A stone memorial to Lenin had just been erected in the middle of the parade field. Cheap Moscow mass production. They never finished the monument to Stalin next to it. Only the legs were there. The rest was in the crate. That's where it'll probably remain.

At the main entrance to one of the opposite buildings was a screamingly colorful *kitsch* portrait. The heads of Lenin and Stalin on the Red flag, surrounded by aircraft, tanks, cannon, and storming Bolsheviks, who overrun black-white border markers. They had conceived of the war differently. There were numerous dead on the grounds. There were even badly wounded in the house, left behind without doctors or help by their comrades. A grisly sight. The "storming" tanks and "thundering" guns, however, have been abandoned and destroyed along the road. In the first three days, 140 tanks and 94 artillery pieces were captured by our armored corps alone. The numbers say it all! Once again, entire regiments were wiped out here as well.

Soviet bombers attacked. Their target was the avenue of advance. Six machines flew directly over the command post. Surprising them, five Messerschmitt fighters were on their necks. An exciting spectacle started. We held our breaths and stared skyward. There was a stream of flame already starting to come out of one . . . it was soon joined by a second. They slammed earthward like fiery-tailed comets. All six machines were set ablaze and shot down. Everything happened as fast as lightning. The fighters were barely in a firing position before the Soviet bombers dove steeply. Only three parachutes slowly made their way to earth. A new attack had the city proper as its target. But only two wooden houses went up in flames. Once again, the fighters were on guard. Two new mushroom clouds of smoke and flame rose skyward after the impacts far to the rear. In a short period, we witnessed fourteen kills. The *Luftwaffe* dominated the skies; it was Mölders and his wing that were guarding us.[3]

Once beyond Bereza-Kartuska, it was the same scene on the road. Knocked-out tanks or abandoned fighting vehicles, whose crews had fled. Once again, gun after gun and limbers and prime movers. There was a blue haze rising from many spots from the thick woods on the other side of the city. The fleeing Bolsheviks were attempting to use the dangerous weapon of fire. They had set the woods on fire. Red flames began to lick their way higher from the bottom of thick pines. Here and there was a dangerous crackling. The moist ground started to smolder. There was no thought of trying to put it out. The only thing that could help was rain. In some spots, flames and hot, dense smoke made their way towards us. But the road was wide.

The march columns pushed themselves forward without letup. Even for us, it was a terrific evocation of German military might. The *Panzerwaffe* has grown ever more powerful. The German artillery is ever stronger. We feel it: A field army with these types of weapons and led by the offensive sprit of the German soldier has to win.

---

3. Translator's Note: Werner Mölders was the first ace in aviation history to claim 100 victories. He commanded *Jagdgeschwader 51* (51st Fighter Wing) at the time of this account. After his 100th "kill," he was withdrawn from active fighter operations and made the inspector general of the fighter forces as an *Oberst*. He died in a *He 111* that crashed in November 1941 as a result of bad weather.

Comparisons with the campaign in France keep popping into our heads. Superficially, it's the same picture. Just as in France, armored columns penetrated deep into enemy territory along the roads. By taking the roads, the great distances are only secondary. The Bolsheviks have fled into the woods by the thousands. But without possession of the lines of communication, they are cut off from the rear and supplies. Their hunger is our ally. It had already driven the first ones into captivity.

White Ruthenia has a large water network. The attack here is a struggle against the waterways. Blown-up bridges over rivers that often have lowlands extending for kilometers on end can hold up the advance for hours, indeed, even days. The road crossed the gigantic bend of the Schtschara twice. The first wooden bridge had not been destroyed. That was thanks to the courageous charge forward of a young tank *Leutnant*. During the night, he rolled over the bridge and advanced farther with his fighting vehicles. The Soviet artillery on the far bank was overrun. Antitank rounds eliminated the guns and crews. At this point, Soviet bombers were attempting to destroy the bridge. The bridge was narrow, and as a result, there was always a dangerous concentration. But the soldiers looked on quietly as the machines dropped their bombs. You could see the bombs tumble out of their bays and estimate where they would fall. The light and heavy *Flak* fired. The little clouds of explosions surrounded the machines. The bomber formations were scattered. The bombs impacted harmlessly in the countryside. The bridge was not hit. Not even later.

A few kilometers farther on, the flaming torch of war hung over the road. The village of Mitowidy was burning. But before we could get there, the alert of "Ambush!" rolled through the column. The vehicles up front had received fire from the right and the left from the woods. Everyone had to stop and veer sharply right. We jumped into the roadside ditch. The edge of the woods was taken under fire with rifles and submachine guns. Armored cars were ordered forward. They went cross-country and let loose with a few bursts in the direction of the woods.

We then moved on. It had turned evening in the meantime. The wooden houses of the village burned like tinder. It looked like a surreal movie set that was burning down. The gigantic flames shone blazing red against the nighttime sky for a long time. Enemy bombers had set a few houses ablaze. The wind took care of the rest.

The upper branch of the Schstschara blocked the continued march. The lead tank and motorcycle infantry elements encountered heavy resistance. The wood line on the far bank of the valley was loaded with guns and machine guns. The middle portion of the bridge had burned up. It was the first destroyed crossing we encountered on the road. Our armored division had to wait a night. The large bridge-laying tanks were made ready.[4] The crossing point would be forced the next day.

After three days, there was a stretch of road behind us that corresponded to the distance from Berlin to Stralsund—one fifth of the way to Moscow.

---

4. Editor's Note: The author may have been referring to the *Brückenleger IV*, a bridge-layer based on the *Panzer IV* chassis. However, all twenty of the completed vehicles were supposed to have been re-converted to the standard *Panzer IV* configuration in late 1940.

CHAPTER 5

Hot Day on the Schtschara

THE ASSAULT OF THE TANKS AND RIFLEMEN

Where the upper course of the Schtschara crosses the main road from Brest-Litowsk to Sluzk for the first time, it is only fifteen meters wide. But the river bottomland extends for some 800 meters with rising sides, so that it resembles a large, flat basin. It is terrain that is open and difficult to cross for an attack in any direction. The meadowlands were a yellowish blooming rug, but they were like all the other waterways in Russia—marshy and treacherous. The road crossed it on an embankment. The bridge had been burned in the middle. A few of the carbonized pilings were still smoldering. The lead elements of the armor corps, which had broken through as far as the Schtschara 200 kilometers out front, had to wait impatiently. It was restricted to the road. There were no detours. The terrain to the left and right of the road was impassable.

The march column consolidated into an armed camp up front. The fighting vehicles, the heavy antitank guns, the howitzer batteries, and the engineers had closed up on both sides of the road. The riflemen, the combat brethren of the tanks, were in the extended woodlands. They were up front, as always, just like the tanks.

The small work table of the division commander was set up behind a blind made out of pines and on which hung a sign: "Do not disturb!" His shot-up armored car was a few meters behind him in the ditch. A direct hit slammed into it just as *Generalleutnant* Model was dismounting the previous day. The artillery regiment commander sat down for a conference with his officers in a shady ditch. The mighty bridgelayer tanks rumbled into the edge of the woods across the way. It was intended to form their steel spans into a bridge for the first time at this location.

The Poles had established a defensive line along the Schtschara against Soviet Russia. The former frontier is quite close. There were several bunkers to the right and the left. They were able to dominate the edge of the woods on the far side with their fires. They had become good observation posts for our artillery. The eyes of the scissor scopes extended over the walls. But the flood plains—from which the crash of impacting rounds and the whip of machine guns echoed until midnight the previous night and from which the flames of the burning wooden bridge flickered—were quiet and peaceful in the sunshine of the early morning. A carefully paddling pneumatic boat appeared behind the high reeds. An officer patrol from the motorcycle infantry was heading out into the land between the lines. We saw the men sneak out once on the far bank. But there were no more rounds being fired. They determined that the Bolsheviks had evacuated their positions during the night in a panic.

The numerous artillery pieces and antitank guns, with which the Bolsheviks had defended the crossing point of the Schtschara the previous day, could be unmistakably identified through the scissor scopes. At this point, they were silent. The rounds from the German fighting vehicles had silenced them. In a tough duel with the enemy artillery, they had emerged victorious.

Next to us, a tank *Leutnant* was observing. He was wearing the Knight's Cross. It was *Oberleutnant* Buchterkirch, the company commander, who had stormed the fire-breathing woodline the previous day as the lead element of the division. In the meadowlands, tankers were in the process of recovering the last of the fighting vehicles that had bogged down in the marshland the previous day. We went forward with the company commander to the bridge. Still caught up in the dramatic fighting of the previous day, his words in the middle of the battlefield make the exciting hours of the assault on the Schtschara come alive again.

The heavy tanks of the lead element rumbled along the *Rollbahn*, the large through-route to the east, at forty kilometers an hour. It was Tuesday, 24 June, the third day of fighting. To the soldiers, it seemed to be that long in weeks. That's how fast the time moves in war. Hill 202, an important piece of high ground near the village of Marynovo to the right of the road, was taken by the tanks and assaulting riflemen. The concentrated fires of the tank main guns quickly finished off the artillery pieces and antitank guns of the enemy.

It was the 2nd Company of our Brandenburg tank regiment that was taking the lead that day, together with the motorcycle infantry. The pursuit rolled on, kilometer after kilometer. Reconnaissance aircraft reported enemy columns pulling back everywhere. The company commander and his tank commanders stood in their open cupolas and observed. They couldn't allow themselves to be off guard for a second. They frequently raised their binoculars to their eyes. The lead elements had advanced far into the enemy sector. The woods next to the road had not yet been cleared. They were full of Bolsheviks. Artillery and antitank-gun rounds could come from any direction at any time. Three enemy tanks attempted to save themselves by fleeing. The 5-centimter main-gun rounds soon caught up with them. Two heavy 21-centimeter guns were abandoned on the road, the last one at the edge of the woods, where the path sank down towards the Schtschara River plain.

A new, important river crossing was in front of the lead company. In the bold, nighttime *coup de main* of a young tank *Leutnant*, the first bridge of the Schtschara bend fell—fifty kilometers to the rear. The same thing had to be tried again—except in the middle of broad daylight. The company commander snuck forward along a woodline and observed. There was no doubt that this valley was going to be defended by the enemy as well. The bridge 200 meters in front of him was still intact. New planks had been put down. There were three trucks on the far side. Had the Bolsheviks brought demolition charges? Up to that point, all of the river crosses along the major route of advance had been taken intact.

A *coup de main* was attempted. The vehicles approached. But the first tanks had barely cleared the concealment of the woodline and rolled towards the flood plain, where they stood out like targets on a range, when garish muzzle flashes lashed out from the far woodline and rounds smacked into the meadowlands, sending black sprays of earth skyward. The Bolsheviks had brought artillery pieces, lots of antitank guns, and heavy machine guns into position on the far woodline. They were well camouflaged and deeply echeloned behind vegetation. They were able to fire at the fighting vehicles over open sights. Improved fieldworks extended along the edge of the woods. The fighting vehicles had to advance quickly across the bridge and shoot the enemy to pieces, if they

hoped to succeed. All four platoons were immediately employed in the
attack. But the vehicles could not disperse properly. The marshy flood
plain next to the road was hardly fighting terrain for heavy tanks. They
could only disperse fifty meters out into the meadowlands on both sides
of the road. That was as far as the soft ground allowed. The *Oberleutnant*
personally moved along the middle of the road along with two other
fighting vehicles towards the bridge. It was an extremely unequal struggle.
The German tanks had to attack over flat ground that sloped downward
and offered no cover.

Firing with everything the main guns and machine guns had, the
steel vehicles rattled towards the enemy's wall of fire. The motorcycle
infantry advanced, using them as cover. They were motorcycle infantry
of the first wave—battle-hardened and tested, the bravest of the infantry!
Overwhelmed by the sudden attack, enemy tanks rolled towards the
bridge—a small armored car with a machine-gun turret and two Christie-
type tanks of the BT variety. They were fast ten-ton vehicles that could
lift up their tracks on the roads and roll on wheels. They wanted to turn
to flee. It was too late. The 5-centimeter main-gun rounds landed in the
middle of their turrets. The one tank lurched in circles. A lance of flame
shot high, and it crashed into the Schtschara. Bursts of machine-gun fire
slammed into the trucks behind it. Wood and glass shattered.

We went up to the tanks. The circular main-gun penetrations were
right under the cannon. The tanks deserved to be proud of their gunnery
skills. The main gun and turret of the other Soviet tank jutted out of the
shallow water. The penetration on it was also right in the middle.

The tank advanced as far as the bridge. The artillery rounds then
started to drum down on the wood. The impacts were also landing hot
and heavy around the fighting vehicles in the meadowlands. Shrapnel and
clumps of dreck banged and smacked against the walls of steel. It was truly
a miracle that none of them was badly damaged. The motorcycle infantry
pressed themselves into the dewy grass and the wet earth. The enemy
batteries were firing a wild final protective fire. In between, there was the
slow *tack-tack-tack* of several heavy machine guns. One antitank round after
the other shot from the barrels into the edge of the woods. Trees split;
branches whirled through the air. There were the flames of exploding
high-explosive rounds. Wherever there was the muzzle flash of the gun,
it was followed by gun parts flying through the air. Direct hit! But in an

area 600 meters on both sides of the road, there were at least two, perhaps three, batteries. The company commander and the tank commanders fighting up front could identify them. It was not possible to get across the bridge in that hail of gunfire. The enemy shot the bridge ablaze. The planks caught fire. Flames were licking at the first pilings.

All of a sudden, the sharper sounds of antitank gunfire started barking between the impacting artillery. Up to that point, they had remained silent. They were a dangerous foe to the tanks. Eight antitank guns were identified.

The orders went out to the gunners over the intercom systems. Most of the tankers in the company were in combat for the first time that day. A baptism of fire initiated by heavy fighting! But they heard the calm voices of their leaders. They helped guard each vehicle. That instills calmness and security. In the din of battle, the radio sets and intercoms are an almost incomprehensible wonder: "Attack! Attack! Don't remain stationary!" The loaders worked feverishly. The gunners traversed on the enemy. The high-explosive rounds were right on target. Fire and clouds of smoke rose high from the edge of the woods. Wood from the trees and the positions flew through the air. The lead fighting vehicles had churned their way in the morass-like soil to within fifty meters of the Schtschara. All of a sudden, the tracks started spinning. Three tanks sunk ever farther into the marshland. The fighting vehicles could neither advance nor pull back.

In the first attack, the enemy in the improved field and woodland positions could not be forced. The fighting vehicles had to pull back into the cover of the woods. The motorcycle infantry also jumped back to the woods.

The fire on the bridge slowly ate away at the thick planks. If the flames could have been extinguished at that point, the crossing would have been secured. The *Oberleutnant* pressed forward to the bridge with a small assault detachment. He reconnoitered the terrain and observed the enemy positions at the edge of the woods in detail. The fire had abated. There were only the occasional artillery shell and a couple of bursts of machine-gun fire. The Bolsheviks must have taken heavy losses. There was movement over there. They were probably evacuating their wounded.

The company commander decided to attack again. Ten fighting vehicles—five echeloned to the right and five to the left—rolled out from under cover one more time towards the bridge. Once again, the motorcycle infantry attempted to work their way to the Schtschara. But the Bolsheviks defended the crossing the point with stubborn tenacity. Once again, devastating fires came from the woods. This time, a battery fired on the right, which had heretofore remained silent. The enemy antitank guns had also not been eliminated entirely. Their sharper sounds could be distinguished from the rest. A few of the vehicles were hit. But the steel front side held. The rounds did not penetrate. The bursts of machine-gun fire whipped across the meadowlands ceaselessly. There was a rapping and beating against the tank armor.

It was impossible for the motorcycle infantry to get to the Schtschara in that fire. They pressed their bodies deeply into the muck, the mush, and the marsh. In that murderous hail of fire, lifting your head was tantamount to death. It was a desperate situation. In this instance, death-defying heroism was to no avail. The motorcycle infantry were unable to move forward or backward. It was worse on the right side of the road. Death swung his scythe ceaselessly above the heads of the assaulting soldiers. The comrades in the meadowlands needed to be gotten out of there. The fighting vehicles moved forward. Lightning and flames spewed from their barrels. They pushed themselves ahead of the motorcycle infantry as cover. It was a difficult rescue operation. But it worked. About twenty minutes passed, but the motorcycle infantry got out without casualties. The machine-gun rounds hammered powerlessly into the steel walls. A small fighting vehicle became immobilized with track problems. Despite the fire, a larger tank started to tow it out. While turning, the small tank revealed its side for a moment. A sharp bang—antitank-gun hit on the side. The vehicle started to burn. But the crew was safe. Up to that point, that was the only total loss.

An important discovery was made in the process. The former Polish bunkers in the fortifications were still being occupied by the Bolsheviks. They were firing in the rear of the assaulting forces with machine guns. The fighting vehicles immediately turned off in their direction. The 5-centimeter main-gun rounds slammed through the gun ports at pointblank range. The riflemen took care of the rest with hand grenades. The bunkers fell silent. The men rested in the woods from the difficult assault. Evening came. The flames on the wooden bridge tongued their way skyward. There was not much chance of saving it anymore.

For the first time, the lead elements got bogged down at a river crossing. Would the enemy succeed in holding up the rapid advance by destroying additional bridges along the avenue of advance? For the time being, it was just the middle portion of the bridge that was burning. The evening sun shone brilliantly red on the banks of clouds. A third attack was attempted so that the division would have an open crossing over the Schtschara the next day. The assault started at 2115 hours. Once again, the 2nd Company of the tank regiment moved out, reinforced by fighting vehicles of the 4th. For the first time, they entered a night engagement. Using their coverage, a company of motorcycle infantry and the 1st Company of a motorized rifle regiment were to cross the river and advance to the edge of the woods.

With their hatches buttoned, their main guns loaded, and new magazines in the machine guns, the tanks trundled down the road and across the meadowlands to the left and right. The riflemen worked their way forward to the river in leaps and bounds with the tanks. They sank up to their knees in the soft ground. The water ran into their boots from above. They dragged pneumatic boats along with them. The tanks fired without interruption. They peppered the entire woodline one more time. The first floats were pushed into the water. Riflemen jumped in. With a few strokes of the paddles, they were across. Then, of course, it was a matter of slow movement, meter by meter. The minutes seemed endlessly long. The rounds from the tanks whistled and screamed above their heads.

Two fighting vehicles of the 2nd Company were once again at the entrance to the bridge. All of a sudden, off to the right, one of the former Polish bunkers fired. In the tumult of battle, it had not been identified previously. Radio orders to one of the fighting vehicles. Its main gun traversed. A few rounds eliminated the enemy to the rear. The company commander jumped down from his vehicle in front of the bridge. He charged forward along with a few riflemen. They took buckets with them. The clambered over the burning, glowing, and smoldering planks and beams. A few of the riflemen worked their way forward to the other side. They remained there, providing security. At that point, there was still no firing aimed at the bridge. Time being of the essence, the soldiers started their difficult efforts to extinguish the fire. Bucket after bucket was dipped into the Schtschara, and the full buckets passed back. The water sizzled. But it was already too late. The fire devoured everything around it. The men may have been at it for about thirty minutes, when the bridge lit up like daylight. The Bolsheviks had discovered our people on the bridge and directed heavy fire on it. The antitank guns started firing again. The wood on the beams splintered.

The work on the bridge to extinguish the fire had to cease immediately. The soldiers pressed themselves flat on the beams that had not already caught fire. With some difficulty, they moved hand over hand or used some gymnastic maneuver to work their way back. But twelve men on the bridge were pinned; they could not move back. Two tanks moved up to the bridge entrance. Protected by them, the twelve men could be evacuated.

On the far side of the river, the leading squads of riflemen had gotten closer to the woodline. There were still separated by about fifty to sixty meters. In front of the woods, however, were dug-out positions, from which machine-gun fire was ceaselessly directed towards them. They took casualties—dead and wounded. The enemy artillery appeared to have been suppressed, however. There were only occasional muzzle flashes lighting up the dark night. But the machine-gun fire continued unabated. They had to pull back again. They carried their wounded with them. A death-defying group was still on the far side of the river. But it also disengaged carefully from the enemy and worked its way back across the river and into the woods. The bridge started burning more intensely; glowing red beams crashed down into the Schtschara.

Nonetheless, the enemy had to evacuate the battered positions during the night. The silence of death lay along the woodland positions. When looking at them, it became clear why they had become untenable after the final attack the previous day. The entire position had been destroyed. It also became apparent how difficult the heroic assault of the tanks and riflemen had been.

We walked along the 600 meters of front. Artillery piece next to artillery piece: howitzers, infantry guns, and antitank guns. In addition, a few meters farther back, the heavy Maxims, still with a belt of ammunition in the feeders. In that narrow stretch, we counted three batteries of four guns each of 12.2-centimeter caliber. Interspersed among them were light and heavy mortars. The antitank guns were skillfully camouflaged with vegetation.

The dug-out trenches and foxholes of the enemy infantry extended in front of the woodline. The impacts of the German rounds were thick in front of the gun and antitank-gun positions. You could see how they hit along the path in the woods and jumped into the guns. Some of the gun shields were torn, the wheels shot out. But the guns that had not received direct hits could also no longer be moved back either. The limbers were piles of rubble in front of and in the woods; the dead horses, ripped apart by the rounds, lay everywhere.

A few meters in the woods, skillfully hidden in the green underbrush, were two armored cars of the latest type. They had also been destroyed. The Bolsheviks had taken heavy losses. Their dead lay everywhere. There were officers, cannoneers, and infantry in the dug-out trenches along the road, all mowed down by machine guns or shredded by direct hits. A wounded Soviet soldier called out to us in German. He was a teacher. The Soviets had taken off shortly after midnight, he said in a fading voice in broken German. There was nothing that could be done for him.

It was an uplifting, proud feeling to look at that position in the woods.

✠

We went back to the road. The 2nd was to be the lead company again today. The recovery of the bogged-down tanks started at first light. All of them could be pulled out of the marshland. The tank company had not lost a single man. It was understandable that the soldiers were in a cheery disposition.

A detour was reconnoitered through the small village to the right of the road. In the meantime, the bridgelayers had rolled up to the Schtschara. The bridging sections had already been assembled. The river is pretty shallow at this location. Without great difficulty, the steel surfaces were placed over the supports from bank to bank. The first tank bridge was ready in ten minutes. It was 1400 hours. The advance on Sluzk continued. To the minute, the lead elements rolled out punctually.

THE HISTORY OF *PANZER-REGIMENT 6*

The regimental history[1] of *Panzer-Regiment 6* records the events of this chapter as follows:

---

1. Translator's Note: Munzel, *Gekämpft, gesiegt, verloren,* 69.

That evening, the 1st Battalion (*Oberstleutnant* Schmidt-Ott) reached the second crossing of the Szczara[2] at Marynowo, but it bogged down there. The bridge over the fifteen-meter-wide river had been blown up and was burning, and the 800-meter-wide marshy bottom land formed an insurmountable obstacle. Detours were not available. The enemy took the German lead elements and the bridge under concentrated artillery fire. When it turned dark, *Generalleutnant* Model arrived at the Szczara and formed an assault detachment under *Oberleutnant* Buchterkirch (commander of the 2nd Company). It was directed to attempt to form a bridgehead during the night. At 2000 hours, the assault detachment—the 2nd Company, elements of the 4th Company, and the light platoon of the regiment along with motorcycle infantry on pneumatic boats—formed up and felt their way forward to the bridge, which was still burning. *Oberleutnant* Buchterkirch jumped down from his vehicle. Together with a few riflemen, he succeeded in crossing the burning bridge under the firing cover of all of the tanks. At the same time, an assault detachment of motorcycle infantry crossed the river in pneumatic boats. The decisive actions of *Oberleutnant* Buchterkirch—critical for the continued advance—were praised in the Armed Forces Daily Report of 6 July. For his actions, he received the Oak Leaves to the Knight's Cross.

After the Szczara bridge was restored by engineers, the advance guard of the *3. Panzer-Division* (*Oberstleutnant* von Lewinski with the 3rd Battalion in the lead) moved out again at 1545 hours on 26 June.

THE DIVISIONAL HISTORY

The divisional history[3] records the events of this chapter as follows:

The *II./Panzer-Regiment 6* continued the attack shortly after 1500 hours as the advance guard. This time, the tanks did not get very far. The second crossing of the Szczara was in front of them. Although the river was only fifteen meters wide, its flood plain extended for more than 800 meters, and with its ascending edges, it formed a proper basin, which was difficult to cross. The bridge, whose freshly cut pilings practically shone to the tank drivers, had been blown up in the middle. There were no routes around at that location, since everything was marshland with the exception of

2. Translator's Note: Geographic names are spelled the same as in the original, even though this is obviously the Schtschara of the firsthand account.
3. Translator's Note: Traditionsverband, *Geschichte*, 112–14.

the road. The remaining elements of the division slowly pushed their way forward. Russian artillery fire and renewed attacks from the air brought continual delays to that approach march and caused casualties. Two *Flak* were completely destroyed.

Generalleutnant Model was unable to stand by in the rear. He had the *2./Nachrichten-Abteilung 39* give him an eight-wheeled radio armored car and rode it to the front. When the general was unable to make further progress due to the congestion on the road, he dismounted to create room. At that moment, a direct hit from an artillery round tore apart the radio vehicle. The four-man crew was killed instantly; *Generalleutnant* Model was unscathed.

The hours passed slowly. Companies from *Kradschützen-Bataillon 3* and the *1./Schützen-Regiment 394* attempted to press forward in the flood plain. The riflemen had to remain close to the road, however, since every step in the blooming meadowlands was a step into mud. The Bolsheviks defended stubbornly in the former Polish bunkers, which had been built years ago as protection against the Soviet Union.

The tanks took the individual bunkers under fire again in order to make it easier for the motorcycle infantry to work its way forward. Finally, a small section was able to make it to the bridge. It was plastered by enemy artillery and cut off. Twelve men were at the bridge and could not get back. The men were not freed from their predicament until friendly fighting vehicles pressed forward, ignoring the enemy's defensive fires.

Fighting had also broken out to the rear of the lead tank elements. Strong elements of the scattered Red detachments had fled into the woods to the right and left of the road and disrupted the following columns with ambushes. As a result, the *I./Schützen-Regiment 3* had to clear the woods at Postolowo in the afternoon. The *3./Schützen-Regiment 3* (*Hauptmann* Peschke) brought back thirty-eight prisoners and one antiaircraft gun.

Towards 2000 hours, *Generalleutnant* Model ordered the *I./Panzer-Regiment 6* to move forward and form a bridgehead. The *2./Panzer-Regiment 6* (*Oberleutnant* Buchterkirch) was reinforced by the regimental light platoon and a platoon from the *4./Panzer-Regiment 6* to execute the mission. The tanks, followed by motorcycle infantry, worked their way forward to the burning bridge by means of aggressive operations.

Oberleutnant Buchterkirch had his men halt there. He personally jumped down from his fighting vehicle. He ran towards the bridge with a few riflemen, while the remaining tanks attempted to break the enemy resistance on the far bank through continuous fire. A few riflemen succeeded in clambering over the burning planks and establishing a foothold on the far side. An assault detachment of motorcycle infantry— using pneumatic boats from the engineer platoon of the *II./Panzer-Regiment 6*—likewise crossed the river. The bridgehead was formed.

Oberleutnant Buchterkirch's actions were praised as follows in the Armed Forces Daily Report of 6 July 1941: ". . . distinguished himself through exemplary bravery! As a result of the fires of the *2./Panzer-Regiment 6*, the Russians lost 2 light armored cars, 6 tanks, 9 antitank guns, and 25 artillery pieces at the second Szczara crossing!"

The bridging column of the engineer battalion was ordered forward that night. Its vehicles encountered an enemy ambush at Milowidy, and one man was wounded. The column reached the Szczara at Minicze intact, however. That placed the engineers one kilometer south of the burning bridge and the bridgehead formed by the motorcycle infantry. Two bridge-laying tanks were brought up to the river at the original location. The placement of the bridge took ten minutes. In the process, a portion of the original bridge was used as support. The second tank drove onto the bridge and placed the second part down to the other bank.

In the meantime, morning had dawned. Russian artillery rounds landed among the elements of the *3. Panzer-Division* that were waiting along the road. This, despite the fact that batteries from *Artillerie-Regiment 75* had moved forward—some of them in open fields near Nibiszcze—and were firing with everything they had. More effective than the artillery were the continuous attacks by Soviet bombers. The armored command vehicle of the *General* was set alight. The fire could be put out quickly, but the driver of the *General, Obergefreiter* Kohlwey, died a few hours later with a head wound.

Towards 1100 hours, the division ordered the continuation of the attack across the bridge that had been built by the engineers. March Group 1 consisted of a reinforced advance guard under the command of *Oberstleutnant* von Lewinski. The advance had to be postponed and did not start until after a two-hour delay. Some of the heavy tanks had to make stops on the bridge, since it was very narrow.

Oberleutnant Buchterkirch rode point again with his company. Behind him were the *3./Aufklärungs-Abteilung 1*, the *5./Artillerie-Regiment 75*, the *1./*

Schützen-Regiment 394, the *I./Panzer-Regiment 6*, the *1./Panzerjäger-Abteilung 543*, the headquarters of *Panzer-Regiment 6* and *Panzer-Brigade 5*, the *1./Pionier-Bataillon 39*, the *II./Artillerie-Regiment 75*, a platoon from *Mörser-Abteilung 604*, the *1./Flak-Regiment 91*, and the *6./Flak-Regiment 59*. The two remaining march groups of the division were led by *Oberstleutnant* Munzel and *Oberstleutnant* Audörsch.

The vehicles rolled through the meadowlands and reached the main road in the vicinity of the bridge. The ruins of the positions, which had been shot up by the *2./Panzer-Regiment 6* the previous evening, could be seen everywhere. There was no stopping *Oberleutnant* Buchterkirch's lead company. The armored vehicles churned their way through the dirt of the road with their heavy tracks. Contact had long been lost with the main body that was following. The company commander left behind a tank at each of the bridges to provide security as he continued east with his fighting vehicles. The *2./Panzer-Regiment 6* was able to reach Filipowicze. The houses of the locality went up in smoke and flames.

CHAPTER 6

Assault against Ambushes

POSITIONS IN THE MARSHES AND WOODS ELIMINATED

Our front was the road. We were driving our powerful lead elements deeper into the Soviet army each day. The enemy to our front . . . in the woods and marshland on both sides of the road . . . and, often enough, to our rear as well. A campaign of ingenious leadership that demanded the most of soldiers in terms of courage and bravery. A war of strong hearts and good nerves. The second crossing over the Schtschara had been forced. It was halfway to the Beresina. There was another 200 kilometers to get that far. There would be two big fights in between, one in front of and the other on the far side of the city of Sluzk.

This is an account of the heroic assault of the riflemen.

The fighting vehicle pushed its way carefully and slowly along the steel supports, which the bridge-layers had placed below the destroyed wooden bridge across the Schtschara. It was a special moment in the big war that we were experiencing. The new engineer technology was employed for the first time. It was a bridge made to order. The advance guard of the *Kampfgruppe* then proceeded to roll across it. A company of fighting vehicles—a company of riflemen in armored personnel carriers, and a company of motorcycle infantry. The combat engineers observed with pride and satisfaction as the advance continued over "their" bridge. It would be many hours before the old wooden bridge would be repaired. It was certainly no small matter when the rapid advance with the steel monsters on the bad roads of Russia was held up—all the greater the satisfaction for a job well done.

The division commander followed the motorcycle infantry in a *Kübelwagen*. He stayed in touch with the advancing company of tanks and the division command post by means of a radio armored car. It was especially necessary in that broken terrain, where the Bolsheviks could attempt ambushes from every patch of woods, that rapid decisions were made. That was proven one more time on this day. The objective was Sluzk, the only small town before Bobruisk on the Beresina. Reconnaissance aircraft had reported that numerous houses were afire since the previous day. The flames could be seen for kilometers. There were columns pulling back everywhere along the roads.

Light antitank guns and heavy machine guns were also on the far side of woods. That was due to the rapid flight of the Bolsheviks after the German tanks and heavy assault guns had eliminated their weapons-studded position along the edge of the woods. A tough-fighting rearguard of regimental strength had to be not too far ahead of us. There were two questions that went through our minds on this move beyond the Schtschara: Would the enemy attempt to resist again? When would our lead elements catch up to the forces in flight? The road to Sluzk rose and fell across the slightly rolling countryside. It was always the same White Ruthenian landscape: patches of woods, groups of trees, knots of vegetation, bushes and brush, meadowlands, and barren ground. Then marshes, nothing but marshland and morass. Gloomily shining water—eerie, depressing, and miserable. The map of this terrain was dominated by the blue of waterways and the marshes, which marked the pathless area that stretched out for kilometers on end. An armored division was chained to the main avenue of advance in this type of terrain.

Fiery torches were ahead of us. Two Soviet tanks and a truck that had been set on fire by the lead tanks. We moved rapidly again, the usual forty kilometers an hour of pursuit. The countryside was silent under the prickly heat of the sun. Didn't we just hear shots chirping above our vehicles ahead? Maybe we were only deceiving ourselves. But keep going fast! Submachine guns and rifle at the ready in our hands. Trucks were burning in the next village with a snap and a crackle. It was Siniawka, whose wooden houses appeared to be empty and devoid of life. There was still a red flag flattering from a gable. Despite our rush, the *Feldwebel* in our *Kübelwagen*, an ethnic German born in the Caucasus, jumped out and ran to the door, blowing it open with a hand grenade, and fetched the faded remnants. According to the red lettering on the building, it was some sort of "Community Building of the White Ruthenian Soviet Republic." A quick look inside. Dirty benches, a small tribunal. On the walls, gaudy posters and a primitive "wall newspaper." It had only gotten to its first edition. A group of women and girls surrounded us outside the house. They overwhelmed us with a lot of chatter. They were Poles, barefoot and dirty to the knees but with lips made up for a night in Paris. They told us how the Bolsheviks had fled the village head over heels the previous day. There were still two wounded Bolshevik aviators in one house; their machine was in a grain field out back. The lance of flame that shot up out of the fuel tank of one of the burning trucks at that moment ended their torrent of words. They fled back into their domiciles with a cry and a screech.

Behind the village, we soon heard lively rifle and machine-gun fire. We had to move the next few kilometers in the cover of the roadside ditch. A nasty, wide stretch of marshland drew straight across to the road from an estate. To the left, it rose to small knolls, which were full of the usual flora: shrubs, brush, and the adjacent woods gave thousands of opportunities to hide and seek cover. The Bolsheviks had set up an ambush there with strong forces. They let the fighting vehicles and the personnel carriers of the first company roll past. They suddenly opened up with well-aimed fire on the motorcycle infantry. An intense engagement developed out of the ambush, lasting until late in the night.

Rounds whipped into the dirt on the road. The rounds sang with bright voices and whistled. In a flash, the riflemen were off their motorcycles. They jumped into position with submachine guns and carbines. A hundred pair of eyes looked for the enemy. Initially, nothing could be identified in the devilish terrain. The Bolsheviks could have been anywhere: behind the bushes on the edges of the miry depression; in the houses of the estate; in foxholes in the middle of the marsh and water; or in the leaves of the trees, where they could not be identified, even at close range. Here and there, there was a muzzle flash; a sand-brown helmet appeared to move. Short bursts of fire were sent in that direction. But the motorcycle infantry could barely show their heads above the cover of the ditch's embankment. Rounds were impacting thickly everywhere. Those could only be coming from snipers with rapid-fire weapons, who were firing from the crowns of trees off to the right in the woods. Of all the opponents whom the German soldier has had to face, the fanatical Soviet soldier is the basest and most sordid, the most devious and insidious of them all. In terms of rawness, he surpasses the Negro from the Congo and Senegal. With a dogged rage, the motorcycle infantry worked their way forward against the invisible snipers in the bushes and trees. Casualties were unavoidable. The first wounded were taken back on the sidecar motorcycles. Two *Messerschmitts* curved over the woods. All of a sudden, a few dark explosions stood out in the clear heavens. The enemy antiaircraft positions could only be a few kilometers away. The two companies that had broken through surely had to be well past them by then.

Without heavy weapons, the motorcycle infantry were unable to advance. Heavy rounds were needed to comb through the thick terrain. The general had long since sent his orders by radio. He took no heed of his person. A tank company rattled forward. It was briefed and then it rolled into position. The turrets traversed right and left. The suspected hedges and vegetation were taken under fire with high-explosive rounds. The next motorcycle company to arrive joined the fray. Flames tongued their way out of the roofs of the scattered outbuildings. The phosphorous munitions lit things on fire rapidly. Whenever muzzle flashes betrayed the positions of the enemy riflemen, the cannonade of the tanks increased. A howitzer went into position twenty meters off the road. Its rounds were fired over open sights and crashed into the wood-line on the other side of the strip of marshland. Fires started in the trees. The crowns broke and branches spun to the ground. There certainly weren't anymore tree snipers there.

The lead companies of the advance guard did not know that a heavy engagement was in progress to their rear. They continued to advance, kilometer after kilometer. Their reports came back on a regular basis. They had passed through the next few villages. Six enemy tanks and two antitank guns had been knocked out. Hours passed. It had become nine in the evening. The general's radio vehicle received a new message: "Enemy tanks and trucks marching in the direction of Sluzk on the road. Attacking. End [of the column] two kilometers in front of me. Own location: Vicinity Ciasnowka." That meant that the lead tanks had advanced a good twelve kilometers farther to the front in the meantime.

Enemy riflemen continued to fire with obdurate stubbornness. The fighting to the south of Murawanka continued. The fighting vehicles of our division came racing forward; the pennant of the commander was on the large command tank. Antitank forces, both light and heavy, unlimbered. Thunderclaps and the roaring of rounds; a heavy howitzer sent a few heavy loads into the woods. But it was impossible to penetrate into the marsh and morass. The general ordered that more combat power be pushed against the ambush position. He was personally leading from his radio vehicle. All of a sudden, a shot of flame came out of the vehicle. Everyone's breath stopped for a heartbeat. Fortunately, however, the signal flare ammunition had only hit the reserve fuel can on the fender and set it alight. The crew was able to quickly extinguish the flames with dirt.

A healthy sense of humor and deadly earnest make good siblings. A small, humorous episode at that dangerous moment: a young artillery *Leutnant* was taking a prime mover to fetch more ammunition for the howitzer. He was right next to the general's vehicle. At that less-than-suitable opportunity, the battery clerk asked his *Leutnant* to sign the daily report. In his excitement, he thundered: "You're coming to me for a signature now? You must be drunk!" He then took off with his rounds. Everyone laughed, most of all *Generalleutnant* Model. "Army life's a great thing, isn't it!" he said. "You need to write about this as well!"

Night fell. The burning houses were a garish red; the flames devoured their old wood and weathered straw greedily. The numerous signal flares with their fiery trails provided a colorful backdrop in the heavens. The German soldier, putting his life on the line in a self-sacrificing manner, contrasted with the stubborn, tough indifference of the Soviet soldier towards life and death. The fire from the Bolsheviks became increasingly weaker. They lay under the trees from which they had fired, shredded and torn apart by the rounds. They defended themselves up to the last meter in their skillfully camouflaged foxholes, which became their graves. There were a few more bursts of machine-gun fire from the motorcycle infantry. The sound of fighting stopped with the fading of hand-grenade detonations. The ambush had been eliminated. The wiped-out remnants may have escaped in the darkness; nothing could be seen. Silence descended over the marshland of Murawanka. The *Kampfgruppe* headed for the lead elements. Left behind were a few crosses above brave motorcycle infantrymen.

The next morning, the tanks approached the burning city of Sluzk. A squadron of heavy bombers pulled back low along the road when we moved out at daybreak. The general again moved with the lead elements. Burned-out tanks and knocked-out antitank guns marked the route of the lead companies once again. Once again, it was a journey filled with tension and the excitement of expected fighting. All along the avenue of advance, the lead elements were once again engaged by enemy riflemen from the woods and the vegetation. Just beyond the former frontier, at the poor, run-down village of Filipowitschi, the losses increased, according to the reports coming from up front. The tree snipers could do little to the steel-skinned tanks, but the officers and soldiers on the prime movers, trucks, staff cars, and other vehicles had to sit there with sub-machine guns and rifles at the ready, screening and observing to the right and the left. The Bolsheviks are sly masters of camouflage and trained for defending from ambush positions. We discovered camouflage jackets and nets, which the riflemen hung in front of their faces. On the elevated road, our vehicles look like targets on a range.

Burning villages and smoldering farmhouses showed where enemy nests had to be smoked out. At especially endangered places, antitank guns and machine gunners cover the columns to both sides. The columns have to move through. Occasionally, the general called for a halt and observed the dangerous, densely vegetated, and impenetrable terrain. It was during one such occasion—still a few kilometers outside of Sluzk—that we were ambushed from the left with a salvo of fire. Several vehicles pulled up behind the right embankment. The general had just dismounted his *Kübelwagen* when the earth on the far embankment shot up. Bullets started whistling around our heads before we could seek cover. Everything happened in a fraction of a second. With a faint cry, the general's driver collapsed. We bedded down the badly wounded man on the thick grass of the embankment. There still appeared to be hope. The general encouraged the man with heartfelt words. He was immediately taken to the clearing station, but the help came too late for him. Shaken, we learned of the death of our brave comrade. All means are justified in war, but this dastardly highwayman tactic made every decent soldier red in the face with rage.

Outside of Sluzk, the flames of war increased. The field howitzers shot the last resistance in the villages and along the city's outskirts to pieces. The city was taken in the morning. The lead tanks immediately moved through it. We approached a wall of smoke. The flames were blazing everywhere from the dry wood. The usual cheap statue of the Chief Bolshevik, Lenin—hollow inside, fragile like plaster, showing him with his goatee, short legs, bare head, and overcoat—was outside of the "House of the Soviet" at the small marketplace in the middle of the sea of flames devouring its way in that direction. A telling symbol in its tawdriness. On the far side of the market place were enemy limbers, horses, and crews torn apart by shells. A couple of miserable figures crept through the burning alleyways, plunderers. The ravenousness of the starving outweighed their fear of death. At the outskirts of the city were new and unscathed military facilities. There were signs of a Soviet military build-up everywhere.

A motorized rifle battalion cleared the city. But the continued march was held up for a couple of hours. The wooden bridge over the small Sslutsch had been blown up. The tireless engineers went to work. But they quickly had to seek cover in the bushes. Antitank rounds slammed into the ground next to them. Along the hedgerow at the closest house was a gun, which was firing down the road. Three fighting vehicles rolled through the shallow waterway and secured the far side. A tank commander, a *Leutnant*, dismounted and reconnoitered on foot. A bullet fired from an ambush cut him down. The tankers clenched their teeth. They would revenge the death of the young leader. The enemy antitank gun was eliminated. A howitzer was brought up in front of the location of the destroyed bridge. The engineers started their work to restore the bridge under its cover. There was a commander's conference at the edge of the airfield at Sluzk. The Fieseler *Storch* could barely land there without crashing, its condition was so bad. The tanks refueled. "We need to move on! At least 100 kilometers. The Beresina is our next objective!"

We moved back into the burning city. The flames still had taken the main road under their control. There were a few business there, the first ones we had seen in Soviet Russia. Soldiers looked around for things to eat or drink. In their flight, the Bolsheviks had to leave everything behind. Even the rolls made out of grayish dough were fresh. What was there to be found in those shops, some of which had two or three display windows? There was vodka by the case. No need for that strong stuff. In this heat, no one could drink it. The soldiers looked for seltzer water. That was the most important thing, since good drinking water was rarer in this country than in Africa. The water in the wells was murky and had to be boiled. But only a few cases of a red, sweet-tasting soft drink were to be found. Then, to our amazement, shelves with sparkling wine—"Soviet Champagne"—as could be read on the labels. There was crab to go with the sparkling wine. Small cans with crab meat written in English, apparently export goods for America. So you could enjoy life in Sluzk after all. Our mistake. Women, who carefully dared to come out of their houses, quickly put us in the know. They were two teachers who had been in Germany before the Great War and spoke German. We had accidently stumbled upon the "restricted distribution point for functionaries." The common people were only allowed to look at this sop from the outside. Besides, there was hardly enough money to shop there. An unspeakable misery was etched on the faces of all of these women. Bolshevism had transformed all into the proletariat and plundered them. The primary school teacher received 320 rubles after all the deductions and forced contributions. A pair of women's shoes cost 400 rubles. There was barely enough for milk, bread, and the occasional cut of meat.

The jumping wind churned the flames like undulating red sheets. A lurid backdrop. Until that very morning, the city had been a witches' cauldron of rumors. The Bolsheviks had already fled the city two days previous to that. The previous day, forces marched back into the city. It was said that War Commissar Voroshilov was personally in Sluzk in order to organize the desperate defense. Warsaw had been conquered back and Berlin had been transformed into rubble and ashes by 600 British and 400 Soviet bombers. There were assemblies and speeches in front of the Lenin statue. That is, until the shout of terror rang out that the Germans were approaching, chasing the Bolsheviks head over heels out of Sluzk.

That evening, the main road was also on fire. The wind was driving the flames into the middle of the road. An eerie sight as the vehicles raced through it. The heat was unbearable. The soldiers had to hold their hands in front of their faces. A gigantic torch illuminated the skies the entire night. There were no dreary window frames that were the home to the horror. The wooden homes were burned down to their foundations. Only the chimneys were left. The city, which had claimed 13,000 residents just a short while ago, was destroyed. Only the stone buildings and the military facilities around Sluzk remained.

From Sluzk forward, the road we were using turned to asphalt. But the face of the terrain remained the same, with the exception that the woods were more numerous, thicker, and more dangerous. Once again, the tanks formed the lead company. This day, they were followed by the first battalion of one of the motorized rifle regiments. The vehicle commanders and platoon leaders in the steel personnel carriers observed the patches of woods with strained attentiveness. Of course, when moving past them quickly, nothing could be identified. There was no doubt that the Bolsheviks were still lurking in the extended stretches of woods. The lead tank elements were thrusting into the Soviet army faster than the Bolsheviks could flee. It was a part of the ingenious campaign planning that the steel wedges drove deeply and quickly into the heart of the Soviet Union, encircled its forces, and then pulled the bands of steel ever tighter around the large sacks.

The first large patch of woods was behind the lead company. Up to that point, not a shot had been fired. Individual concrete-block houses on both sides of the road appeared abandoned. The villages were empty. The residents most likely had fled into the woods, as they usually did. Lonely and desolate.

"Panzer marsch!"

The first tank moved out again—as always, in the direction of the Beresina. But it was in those woods that the Bolsheviks had set up their second large ambush. When the second and third companies rolled up, they received murderous fire. Devastating machine-gun fire rattled against the vehicles from point-blank range. Those were a terrible few seconds. Before the riflemen could jump into position and take cover, there were heavy casualties—dead and wounded. They took up the fight with rage and wrath and an exemplary disdain of death. They were battle-hardened soldiers with the tradition of an old regiment from Hamburg. They had been in Poland, fought in the Dyle Position, assaulted into the pocket at Dunkirk, and broken through the Weygand Line. Their battalion commander, *Major* Kratzenberg, was a recipient of the Knight's Cross.[1]

The patch of woods was a fire-spitting hell. Innumerable submachine guns and automatic weapons showered the German assault soldiers with a hail of bullets. But they worked their way towards the woods. Heavy fire traveled down the length of the cut in the woods. The Soviets were

---

1. Translator's Note: Kratzenberg was the commander of the *III./Schützen-Regiment 3*, when he received the award for his actions in France (awarded 15 August 1940). He survived the war and passed away on 24 January 1976 in Bad Oldesloe.

sitting in deeply dug-out positions under the trees, camouflaged with leaves and pine needle branches. You could hardly even see the heads of the Bolsheviks. The riflemen of the two companies attacked with the exemplary bravery that has always characterized the German infantryman as the best in the world. They moved out against the ceaselessly hammering machine guns. The platoon leaders in front were a shining example of duty unto death. Platoon leaders were killed. The soldiers assaulted across the dead. Whenever a comrade fell, another one's courage was doubled. The battalion commander was wounded, as was a company commander. In the rain of bullets, the young *Unterarzt* pressed his way to the wounded. He was also killed. Medics were killed trying to evacuate the wounded. But the great sacrifice was not in vain. The woods were stormed. Each one of the men who fought and bled there was a hero. That proud word is not too much to characterize what they did. Those were heroic deeds that were done by the dead, the wounded, and the living.

We went through the woods and looked at the many-branched defensive system. A Soviet officer was squatting only thirty meters from the street, in a small, narrow foxhole that was just big enough to let him in. It was under low-hanging pine branches, and he could not be seen until you were standing right in front of him. A German hand grenade had killed him, just like all these Soviet soldiers, who were lying pale and silent next to their weapons. There were automatic and modern rapid-fire weapons everywhere, cans full of ammunition and hand grenades and small mines. On the field path towards the rear, there was a tractor with a heavy gun. Rounds had set the fuel tank on fire. The crew lay next to the vehicle, burned to death.

In front of the woods where they charged, emerged victorious, and died were the dead of the 1st Battalion. Their comrades addressed their final needs. All of us were quiet and moved. It became the first large cemetery on the road to victory. The regimental physician personally buried the young *Unterarzt*. He had tears in his eyes, as did many others. No one needed to be ashamed of that. They are hard soldiers. That day had made them even harder. The fight against Soviet Russia is a difficult one. But every soldier knows that it needs to be fought to the end so that Germany can live. A cross rose high above the many smaller crosses with the names on them. A young comrade spoke softly:

> If one of us should fall,
> The other one stands for two,
> Because God gave every fighter
> A comrade to go with him.

It seemed as though that verse stood invisibly above the grave marker.

The houses and the villages around the contested woods had to be cleared. Tracer ammunition from the light *Flak* caught fire in the straw-thatched roofs. Once again, the night was illuminated by fire.

As on the previous day, the tanks led the *Kampfgruppe*. The brigade commander was in front. The *Kampfgruppe* covered kilometer after kilometers without incident. The objective—the Beresina—grew ever closer. But before that, a tributary of the Pripet had to be crossed, the Ptitsch. A long wooden bridge led across it. When the first tanks rolled up, flames shot out of the wood. The Bolsheviks had placed hay in the gaps, poured gasoline on it, and set it on fire. It was a wild scene, the young signal officer in the command vehicle reported to us the next day.

"Keep moving!" the brigade commander ordered. Tanks started to provide covering fire and sent a few high-explosive rounds on the heels of the fleeing firebugs. The fighting vehicles moved through the tongues of flames to the far bank. The planks had already burned, but the thick beams underneath held. It rattled and shook; the crews were tossed about. On the far side, antitank guns were firing. The cannon tanks[2] quickly sent a few rounds that way. Three command vehicles and five tanks completed the dangerous ride across the burning bridge. Four personnel carriers still had to go across. The flames were already shooting meters into the air. Would the beams hold out?

The personnel carriers also completed the difficult trick. But the vehicles were open on top. The flames hit inside and crews' things caught fire. The rubber pads on the tracks burned. The flames were extinguished with fire extinguishers. The soldiers beat on the burning items to put them out. Fire extinguishers were used in an effort to put the fire out on the burning bridge. But the effort was in vain. The entire bridge was a seething fire by then. An hour later, it collapsed on itself. But the lead

---

2. Translator's Note: The author is referring to the *Panzer IV* with the short (L/24) 7.5-centimeter main gun, which was still the heaviest weapon mounted on a German tank at the time.

tank continued moving. It thought the other vehicles were behind it. The radioed orders did not reach it. It advanced until just right outside of Brobruisk. At that point, it noticed it was alone on the road. On the way back, it was approached by two enemy tanks and a truck. That was a nasty surprise for the Bolsheviks. Before they could fire, the German tank had taken care of them.

The next morning, the engineers were brought forward again. But, of course, the terrain in front of the Ptitsch is also marshland. One waterway here is the same as the next one. A corduroy road was built. The men were fetched out of the villages and put to work. In the meantime, a detour had been found, although it was a badly worn-out road. Other than the main road, the paths and trails here have no shoulders and are almost impassable. The column churned its way forward through knee-deep sand. A few vehicles became stuck. Prime movers and trucks with three axles pulled the bogged-down ones free. Fortunately, the bridge over the Ptitsch in the village bellow the main route of advance was intact. The advance continued across it to the main road in the direction of Brobruisk on the Beresina.

The first tanks rattled over the cobblestones of the dead city. The riflemen of the 1st Company worked their way to the river. Once again, a difficult fight ensued for an important river crossing. The never-ending ribbon of the army columns rolled behind them. All engines and all hearts beat only one word: Forward!

THE HISTORY OF *PANZER-REGIMENT 6*

The regimental history[3] of *Panzer-Regiment 6* records the events of this chapter as follows:

After the Szczara bridge was restored by engineers, the advance guard of the *3. Panzer-Division* (*Oberstleutnant* von Lewinski with the 3rd Battalion in the lead) moved out again at 1545 hours on 26 June. The regimental headquarters and the 1st Battalion (*Oberstleutnant* Schmidt-Ott) reached a large section of woods towards evening. They moved through it and closed up with the 3rd Battalion (*Hauptmann* Schneider-Kostalski) to the front. All of the wheeled elements had to remain behind, since the woods were still heavily occupied. At that point, the 2nd Battalion, which belonged to the second march group, positioned its tanks on the left and right

---

3. Translator's Note: Munzel, *Gekämpft, gesiegt, verloren*, 69–70.

sides of the road to provide security. They kept the invisible enemy in the woods under suppressive fire and thus enabled the wheeled vehicles to be channeled forward. Despite that, there were casualties in the darkness. For instance, the leader of the messenger section of the 2nd Battalion, Dressler, a college preparatory school graduate, was killed when he followed the command vehicle of his commander, *Oberstleutnant* Munzel, despite being ordered not to do so. The battalion physician, Dr. Zülch, was wounded when he left his armored ambulance to render first aid to the wounded.

All elements of the regiment reached Filipowitschi around 0200 hours on 27 June. They formed a "hedgehog" position there. They moved out again at 0525 hours, after refueling. The 3rd Company reached the city of Sluck[4] around 1000 hours as the lead element. After a sharp engagement, in which the entire 1st Battalion was involved and *Oberleutnant* Vopel of the 1st Company especially distinguished himself, the battalion took the city, which was burning in many places, along with the regimental headquarters, which was on the left wing. Collapsed houses blocked the streets in some instances. All of the bridges east of the city had been destroyed. During the effort of the 1st Company to go around the city to find a crossing point over the river farther north, *Leutnant* Max von Kiekebusch was killed by a sniper, who fired at him from a tall cornfield. In the period from 24 June until 1600 hours on 27 June, the regiment had covered a distance of approximately 150 kilometers from Bereza, while fighting to the east.

After supply vehicles reached Sluck in the course of the night, the continued advance was ordered for 0815 hours on 28 June. This time, it was the reinforced 2nd Battalion in the lead. It was followed by the regimental headquarters and the 1st Battalion. The day's objective was established as the city of Brobruisk on the Beresina. After just a few kilometers, the 5th Company encountered the enemy. The same situation had repeated itself. Although the lead elements had overrun the enemy and destroyed two artillery pieces, the unarmored vehicles that followed got bogged down in heavy fire. In the thick woods near Kalista, the enemy was once again almost invisible. He engaged the vehicles and motorcycle messengers from well-camouflaged field positions. There were high casualties among the riflemen, the engineers and the artillerymen. A

---

4. Translator's Note: The city of Sluzk in the firsthand account.

long halt ensued. Under the leadership of the division commander, a
few assault detachments, which also had members of the regimental field
trains and the regimental headquarters and battalion headquarters added
to them, pressed into the woods on both sides of the road. Suffering
casualties, they drove the Russians out, who had offered strong resistance.
In the meantime, *Generalleutnant* Model had formed a "tank convoy"
out of the tanks of the regimental light platoon and the 1st Battalion
and placed a tank every 50 to 100 meters along the right and the left
of the road. Heading east, the vehicles moved out again at a fast pace
at 1600 hours. Whenever resistance flared up again, the tanks fired with
everything they had into the woods while the field trains of the regiment
and the wheeled vehicles of the division followed between them. Suffering
minimal casualties, the rail line at St. Dorchi was reached at a fast pace
at 1800 hours. Fortunately, the woods thinned out there and contact was
reestablished with the lead elements of the division about ten kilometers
west of Brobruisk at 2140 hours.

In the meantime, the 2nd Battalion and its lead element (5th
Company) had reached a burning road bridge over the Ptitsch. Eight
tanks and four armored personnel carriers were able to get across the
bridge before it collapsed. The brigade commander, *Oberst* Linnarz,[5] who
was riding up front, attempted to put the fire out on the bridge with a
few people. The elements coming up from the rear thought they were
Russians. The lead tank fired, badly wounding the brigade commander
and ultimately costing him one of his arms.

Late in the afternoon, the division commander also reached the lead
elements of the advance guard outside of Brobruisk. He ordered the
immediate attack by all tanks on Brobruisk. As a result of the destroyed
bridge over the Ptitsch, small, unimproved roads south of the main road
had to be used. They very quickly proved almost impassable due to the
frequent cloudbursts that day. The smaller bridges collapsed and were
either repaired in a field-expedient fashion by the tank crews or bypassed.
With some difficulty, a few of the tanks that had been held back towed
through the water and the marsh the badly needed supply vehicles with

---

5. Translator's Note: After losing his arm, Linnarz went on to a number of staff
positions, eventually being promoted to *Generalleutnant.* He ended the war commanding the *26. Panzer-Division* in Italy for the final months of fighting in 1945.

fuel and ammunition. The regiment spent the night in the sluggish advance and struggled slowly to the vicinity of Brobruisk.

It was not until 0345 hours on 29 June that the 2nd Battalion entered the city of Brobruisk on the west bank of the Beresina against weak enemy resistance. The battalion's light platoon raised the German flag over the citadel right on the river. The bridges, however, had been destroyed by the enemy. The riflemen cleared the city. The regiment moved into a few of the smaller villages west of the city.

THE DIVISIONAL HISTORY

The divisional history[6] records the events of this chapter as follows:

Around 0525 hours on 26 June, orders came from the brigade to continue the march. The objective was Sluzk! The advance guard moved out in the same order as the previous day. The *2./Panzer-Regiment 6* moved along the road without stopping. To the north of the village of Gulicze, a Russian antitank gun position caused a temporary halt. But the resistance was quickly broken and the march continued. *Oberleutnant* Buchterkirch rattled east with his fighting vehicle. The turrets of the city of Sluzk appeared on the horizon. The tanks were two kilometers from the locality at that point.

All of a sudden, there was a howling from all sides. The Soviets intended to defend Sluzk. On orders from the headquarters of the Western Front, they had brought artillery and antitank guns into position in order to force a stop to the German advance at all costs. The *2./Panzer-Regiment 6* was unable to make any further advance. *Oberleutnant* Buchterkirch dismounted and rallied the riflemen forward across an embankment. Fortunately, the 1st Battalion, which was following, soon closed up. Since the terrain on both sides of the road was passable to armor, *Major* Schmidt-Ott had his battalion approach across a broad front. The fighting vehicles took the identified Russian positions under fire and held down the defenders until the *5./Artillerie-Regiment 75* (*Oberleutnant* Grigo) arrived and took out the enemy batteries. A short while later, the *1./Schützen-Regiment 394* arrived with its armored personnel carriers. Towards 1100 hours, orders were issued for an attack.

The *1./Panzer-Regiment 6* (*Oberleutnant* Vopel) advanced into the city without delay. Although the Russians offered resistance at several spots,

---

6. Translator's Note: Traditionsverband, *Geschichte*, 115–18.

they were surprised by the energetic attack of the lead armor elements. The wooden houses burned and collapsed like blazing torches. On more than one occasion, the fighting vehicles had to find a way around or over the rubble. The moved rapidly through the small market place, where the Lenin memorial rose up in the middle of the sea of fire. Soviet vehicles were on the opposite side of the plaza, the crews and horses shredded by rounds. But the tank drivers didn't have any time to take that in; they continued the assault on and past the new military facilities on the outskirts of the city. Suddenly, the fighting vehicles had to halt. The wooden bridge over the small Sslutsch at Wiesiekja had been blown up. The vehicles with the engineers immediately rolled forward. Enemy antitank guns opened fire on and near the bridge and did not allow the engineers to approach. The fighting vehicles moved upstream and downstream in an effort to find a ford. In the process, *Leutnant* von Kiekebusch (*1./Panzer-Regiment 6*) was felled by a Russian sniper on the far bank.

The *I./Schützen-Regiment 394* (*Major* Kratzenberg) had moved up to Sluzk and cleared the burning city of the remaining Soviet forces with all of his companies. Sluzk was a gigantic mass of flames. They were fed by the wind which, in turn, had resulted from the large fires. The last Russian soldiers were fetched from their hiding places by noon. The few civilians hastened through their burning city, shy and agitated, and attempted to plunder the few businesses. The soldiers of *Schützen-Regiment 394* were able to capture the equipment stores in the military facilities and distributed food items, bread, flour, and butter to the residents, who had been without food for two days. The battalion then moved east of the city and secured.

Up to that point, the *3. Panzer-Division* had only assaulted along one road. As a result, there was an immense length to the entire column. The lead elements bore themselves like an arrow into the enemy front. But the Soviets were sitting in the woods and marshland to the left and the right and did not even consider the prospect of surrendering. They attacked the supply convoys that followed again and again and inflicted considerable casualties. Correspondingly, *Schützen-Regiment 3* (*Oberst* von Manteuffel) was given the mission of screening the route of advance. The *I./Schützen-Regiment 3* screened in the area Kantonowicz–Janowicze on 26 June. To the left was the division field replacement battalion in the area around Siniawka. *Aufklärungs-Abteilung 1* was around Kleck. The outposts remained where they were until late in the afternoon. At that point, the lead elements of the *4. Panzer-Division* had arrived. The regiment took off after the division, which had hurried far ahead.

The lead elements were already some 300 kilometers from the borders of the *Reich* and had covered a fifth of the entire distance to Moscow. That stretch had left its mark on men and materiel. The vehicles rattled from top to bottom, the weapons were covered in dust and the soldiers overly tired.

Generalleutnant Model arrived in Sluzk shortly after noon and called his commanders together at the former airstrip. He scolded the march discipline of the forces. That not only caused delays in the advance, it also offered enemy aircraft good targets.

"We have to move on! The Beresina is our next objective . . . and then Moscow is in front of us!"

There was no more advance that day. The Russians continued to block the riverbanks. It was not until the friendly artillery could be brought forward to provide covering fire that a new bridge could be built. At least the forces were able to use the transition to screening to clean some of the dirt and sand from their weapons and attend to the damage on the vehicles. The division surgeon established a main clearing station in the orphanage in Slulz with *Sanitäts-Kompanie 522*.

The division ordered the continuation of the advance at 0730 hours on 27 June. The advance guard formed two march serials to that end: one under *Oberstleutnant* von Lewinski and the other under *Oberstleutnant* Munzel. The tank regiment assembled at the outskirts of the city. The reconnaissance aircraft had noted hardly any enemy movement along the road to Brobruisk. It was assumed that rapid progress would be made that day. At least that's what the men of the *3. Panzer-Division* thought that morning.

While taking its midday rest, the *1./Panzerjäger-Abteilung 543* was attacked by scattered Soviet forces. The 1st Platoon immediately took up firing positions, while *Oberleutnant* Michels and ten volunteers advanced against the approaching tanks. In a short engagement, the antitank men were able to eliminate five enemy fighting vehicles. Afterwards, it was determined that the tanks in question were command tanks with valuable materiel on board, including papers, documents, 5,000 meters of film, women's silk clothing (!), and other things.

The *5./Panzer-Regiment 6* (*Oberleutnant* Jarosch von Schweder) took the lead, after the Sslutsch had been crossed. The tanks made good progress on the road, but they received fire after a few kilometers from some high ground that ran perpendicular to the road. The Russians had dug in artillery and antitank guns there. The *5./Panzer-Regiment 6* deployed north of the road into attack formation and broke the enemy resistance after a short period. Two cannons fell into German hands. *Panzer-Regiment 6* moved out again to continue the march at 1200 hours. After a short while, there were the first hold-ups in the march. The lead elements had run into a Russian position in the woods around Stary-Hutok. That resistance was also broken rapidly, and the tanks continued to roll on through the woods and isolation.

After the fighting vehicles had passed the dangerous spot, it suddenly turned lively in the woods around Kalista, when the riflemen, engineers, *Flak* gunners, and cannoneers followed. As if on command, heavy, rapid fire from machine guns and automatic weapons broke out of the impenetrable thickets from all sides. The riflemen quickly threw themselves on the ground from their vehicles, seeking cover. Minutes passed that seemed eternally long. Friendly tanks rolled forward from the rear. It was the lead elements of the *I./Panzer-Regiment 6*. The fighting vehicles moved their way carefully along the wooded road. They were also showered with a hail of fire, but those rounds ricocheted off. *Generalleutnant* Model was in the middle of that group. He stood upright in his open staff car and attempted to organize a defense from there. He summoned the commander of the *I./Schützen-Regiment 394*. When *Major* Kratzenberg approached the general, he sank to the ground, badly wounded. *Hauptmann* Orts then assumed command. But he also collapsed, hit twice in the legs. He died soon afterwards at the main clearing station. *Oberleutnant Freiherr* von Werthern then assumed command of the battalion. Nothing could be seen of the enemy, but heavy fire was coming from the woods. *Oberleutnant* von Werthern issued orders: "Fix bayonets! Get up . . . go . . . go!" The fight with the well-camouflaged opponent was conducted with determination on both sides. Every individual mound of earth, behind which a Russian had dug in, had to be stormed. The enemy defended strongly and could only be eliminated in close combat or by means of hand grenades. The woods around Kalista were then in the possession of the *I./Schützen-Regiment 394*. It was a major success. Unfortunately, it had been bought with heavy casualties. *Leutnant* Berg, *Leutnant* Nebel, and *Leutnant* Bley fell at the front of their platoons. *Leutnant* Rougemont received a dangerous stomach wound; he died a few hours later. *Stabsarzt* Dr. Marr had his hands full. The young *Unterarzt,* Kalten, was with the riflemen, who were slowly clearing out one pocket of resistance after the other. The medic, *Unteroffizier* Sprössing, was wounded. *Unterarzt* Kalten went to help dress his wound and was mortally wounded.

Generalleutnant Model had witnessed the fighting of his soldiers while standing on the road and had personally issued directives and orders. When the fighting came to a conclusion, the general was able to thank the badly wounded *Major* Kratzenberg one more time for the accomplishments of his brave battalion. *Hauptmann* Pape of *Kradschützen-Bataillon 3* assumed command of the *I./Schützen-Regiment 394.* For his brave and actions, *Oberleutnant* von Werthern was later award the Knight's Cross.[7]

The division commander then had a convoy formed from the fighting vehicles of the *I./Panzer-Regiment 6.* They escorted the unarmored vehicles through the woods. The light platoon of the tank regiment took the lead in order to establish contact with the *II./Panzer-Regiment 6,* which had ranged far ahead. The remaining tanks were positioned at 100-meter intervals to the left and right of the road to allow the vehicles through. The peculiar type of advance started around 1600 hours.

In the woods around Kalista, however, the work of the doctors, medics, and chaplains continued. Fresh graves were dug. Forty-three officers, noncommissioned officers, and enlisted personnel were given over to eternal rest under the trees and brush. In the evening, a large wooden cross was erected. The two divisional chaplains, Laub and Dr. Heiland, held the funeral remarks, along with the regimental commander, *Oberstleutnant* Audörsch.

In the meantime, the *II./Panzer-Regiment 6* (*Oberstleutnant* Munzel) had continued its advance, despite the fighting that had brewed up behind it. Right in front of the bridge over the Oressa, the enemy had set up an obstacle with destroyed armored vehicles. When friendly fighting vehicles showed up, they received a hail of well-aimed artillery fire. The *5./Panzer-*

---

7. Translator's Note: Von Werthern received the Knight's Cross on 8 September 1941. He ended the war as an *Oberstleutnant* and went on to serve in the *Bundeswehr,* where he retired as an *Oberstleutnant.* He passed away on 10 January 2001 in Großhansdorf (Hamburg).

Regiment 6, moving in front, stopped briefly. *Feldwebel* Noelte moved up to the obstacle with his tank and collapsed it with the weight of his steel colossus.

Oberst Linnarz personally took the lead in the command vehicle of his brigade headquarters. They were closely followed by the 7th and 5th Companies of *Panzer-Regiment 6*. Kilometer after kilometer, the tanks churned their way forward through the roads, which had been softened by cloudbursts early in the afternoon. Then they were in front of the Ptitsch, a small tributary of the Pripjet. There was a long wooden bridge over the water at Gluscha.

Oberst Linnarz did not hesitate long. He ordered an immediate crossing. The beams on the bridge started to burn. The fighting vehicles moved through the tongues of flame to the far bank. The planks on the bridge soon went up; only the beams remained. The three command vehicles and the five tanks were already across. Right behind them, the four armored personnel carriers with the riflemen attempted to get across. They succeeded. Then, with a mighty crack, the bridge collapsed.

By then, the tanks of the *7./Panzer-Regiment 6* were at the river. *Leutnant* Rühl saw movement on the bridge and thought he had Russians in front of him. The vehicle of the brigade commander was inadvertently knocked out, in the process of which *Oberst* Linnarz lost his right arm. *Oberstleutnant* von Lewinski assumed acting command of the brigade.

The following elements of the tank regiment closed up. But there was no getting over the river in the dark night. *Generalleutnant* Model, who had ordered the attack on Brobruisk at 2100 hours, immediately ordered *Aufklärungs-Abteilung 1* to reconnoiter south for a detour. The armored cars finally located a badly worn-out road. The columns then churned their way forward through the knee-deep sand. The route was marshy in spots; as a result, some of the wheeled vehicles became stuck. They could only be pulled out of the muck by means of prime movers and tanks. A small bridge broke under the weight of the trucks, but it could be repaired for the time being.

Banks of fog continued to lay over the countryside, when the engines of the tanks sprang to life. They slowly pushed forward into the first outlying settlements of Brobruisk. Nothing stirred; only individual flames shot out of some of the huts. Friendly artillery had sent out its fiery greetings the previous evening. The light platoon of *Panzer-Regiment 6*, the light platoon of the *I./Panzer-Regiment 6*, and the armored personnel company of *Schützen-Regiment 394* took the lead. The fighting vehicles rattled at speed over the roads. The squalid wooden houses and edifices of the party remained behind. There was hardly any resistance. It was only at the old citadel that the enemy put up a defense. The resistance was broken when all of the weapons in the lead element were brought to bear. At 0450 hours, the men of the light platoon of the *I./Panzer-Regiment 6* raised the *Reich* war flag on the turret of the citadel. Brobruisk had been taken!

Our tanks advanced into the artillery positions along the Beresina.

The destroyed bridge over the Beresina. Despite the apparent and extensive damage, this bridge could be repaired and rendered usable relatively rapidly by engineers, since most of the spans are still intact.

Traffic continues across on ferries to the burning shore. A prime mover can be identified on the lefthand ferry.

The temporary bridge is finished. The first German tanks rolls across the Beresina. The tank seen here is a *Panzer III*, recognizable by the distinctive silhouette of its main gun. The tank has to move at a walking pace, since the bridge will support the weight, but it is not stable enough to withstand crossings at standard road speeds.

Prisoners stream to collection points from all sides.

Civilians lead their herds back, protected by the German Armed Forces.

Soviet trucks serve as torches along our avenue of advance.

The enemy puts up tough resistance in the woods. This is most likely a machine-gun section, since the soldier on the right has a belt of ammunition draped over his shoulder.

A poor road makes you inventive. These soldiers are making use of what would become known as the *panje* cart. The *panje* was a small but strong and durable Russian draught horse. This type of transportation was often the only way to move along the notoriously bad Soviet road network during inclement weather.

The division commander, *Generalleutnant* Model, receives a report.

In 1939, the Soviets occupied eastern Poland. There are still improved roads there. Much of the initial fighting took place before the actual Soviet border was reached. In this image, we see an early *Panzer IV* in "campaign mode," as evidenced by the additional stores placed on its rear deck and the mounting of a spare roadwheel on the rear hull. The thin, sheet-metal mudguards have also suffered damaged, most likely as the result of bumping into vegetation or manmade objects.

A heavy mortar section changes position during fighting in a built-up area. The soldier on the left carries the mortar tube, while other members of the crew carry their respective parts of the weapon. Note the application of field-expedient camouflage in the form of vegetation to some of the helmets.

Concealed in a buckwheat field, an artillery forward observer calls in enemy positions. His comrade reports the fire effect to the command post.

CHAPTER 7

Across the Beresina
and the Dnjepr

BRIDGEHEAD AFTER A HARD FIGHT—VICTORIOUS AIR BATTLE OVER BROBRUISK

In six days, German armored forces advanced more than 400 kilometers on the road to Moscow from Brest-Litowsk, going straight through White Ruthenia along the Rokitno and Pripet Marshes. At Brobruisk, the road crosses the Beresina, the river that brought a decisive defeat to the fleeing army of Napoleon in 1812. In the Great War, the Beresina also had a role to play. It was the river where the German and Austrian forces stood when the peace negotiations were initiated in Brest-Litowsk. Perhaps the Bolsheviks believed they would experience a turning point along the Beresina in 1941, just as the French had also believed in a "miracle of the Marne" in 1940. Shortly before the German forces arrived at the west bank of the Beresina, Voroshilov and Timoschenko personally stayed in Brobruisk in order to organize the defenses against the German armored advance. The terrain provided their intent with all sorts of advantages. The Bolsheviks could construct good defensive positions behind the 100-meter-wide river, which flowed through marshy meadowland.

When the lead German elements reached the Beresina at Brobruisk, they were greeted with artillery fire. For the time being, a crossing was out of the question, since the Bolsheviks had strong forces on the far bank and the bridges over the river had been blown up. It was clear to the command structure of *Generalleutnant* Model's division advancing along the road— based on battle impressions, prisoner statements, and the results of aerial reconnaissance that were brought back—that the Bolsheviks would attempt with all the means at their disposal to stop the further advance of the Germans at the Beresina. Every single day that the German crossing of the

Beresina was delayed was an immeasurable win for the defenders, whose front was constantly being reinforced by forces being brought up from central Russia.

On the tank route that the division had used, the vehicles of the lead division assembled on the right side of the road. The artillery rolled past them to the front. They first had to soften up the Bolsheviks and silence their batteries before the engineers and the infantry, followed by the tanks, could be employed. The artillery observers established their positions in the citadel of Brobruisk, which rose right on the water with its fifteen-meter-high walls. The scissor scopes were carefully raised above the edge of the old green wall. The observations posts were right in the front lines along with the companies of a rifle regiment. Their vehicles had been brought forward to the cover of the military buildings of the citadel and camouflaged. The enemy shells exploded with hard blows in the courtyards and on the buildings, on the walls, and in the trenches of the old fortress. The rushing of the shells, the crash of the impact, the howling of the shrapnel, and the shattering of the windowpanes, combined with the rumbling of the vehicles that sought cover somewhere at full speed— those were the sounds that echoed in the old citadel.

The blast waves of the exploding shells ripped sheets of metal off the roofs in the military facilities. They whirled through the air and crashed with a bang into the plaster. The air was oppressively hot and humid. The senses of those who had to go into position on the higher west bank of the Beresina were on high alert. They worked their way forward to the edge of the banks until they had a good view and fields of fire to the far side, where the enemy was set up everywhere in the broad, green river valley. They could be seen quite clearly crawling around in the vegetation along the river and in the tributaries. You could see the Bolshevik infantry assault detachments work their way right up to the water . . . how they dug out shallow foxholes and brought up ammunition with them.

There was feverish work at the measuring centers of the ranging batteries, which were creating the basis for a decisive fire-for-effect of the artillery. All of the identified strongpoints and positions of the enemy were entered on the maps. The firing plans were created after the maps were marked; they would be used to direct the fire of the individual batteries. That afternoon, after the columns of combat forces had closed behind the one-story houses of Brobruisk and taken up positions that offered concealment from the air—and taken in a quick bite to eat from the field kitchens—a severe storm let loose on the Beresina Valley with lightning, rolling thunder, and cloudbursts of rain. The entire river landscape became blurry in the haze. It was almost impossible for the observation posts on the citadel to identify anything. The Bolshevik artillery continued to fire round after round into the old walls. Enemy patrols used the haze, which hung like fog in the river valley, to cross over to the west bank of the Beresina on the ruins of one of the demolished bridges and on rowboats. The machine guns of the riflemen in position along the wall rattled and forced the Bolsheviks to ground. The section on the bridge pulled back rapidly, taking casualties. In the citadel, the artillerymen had to resort to carbines and submachine guns, however, to keep from being surprised.

After the weather had abated, the tension had also been scaled back. The Bolsheviks had not made it through. They had also not succeeded in establishing themselves on the near side of the river. The danger had been turned back, but in its place there appeared bombers over the city on the Beresina. The *Flak* had its hands full. All of the light and heavy guns bellowed whenever the Red Star appeared on the horizon. With their rounds, which appeared like large black dots in the skies, they scattered the enemy's flight formations and prevented the Bolshevik aviators from conducting an aimed drop of their bombs on the approach routes to Brobruisk and the positions along the Beresina.

Disregarding the enemy artillery and aerial activity, the German batteries, which accompanied the tanks during their advance, went into position. One after the other, they opened fire and sent their rounds into the woods on the far side of the river. The fight along the Beresina for a crossing point was in full gear.

The German mechanized forces were struggling to gain control of a crossing over the Beresina River. They did not want to be held up in their vigorous, rapid advance east despite the considerable Bolshevik defensive measures. On the other side, the Bolsheviks did everything in their power to stop the German advance at any cost along this natural obstacle. In the fight for the bridge locations along the Beresina, scenes emerged that one had rarely seen in modern warfare.

You could practically follow every combat arm in its battle and likewise identify the measures of the enemy on the far side of the river. The artillery fight continued thunderously. The engineers sent their first reconnaissance teams forward to look for a suitable place to build a bridge. The riflemen in the forward lines received reinforcements, while the approach march of the German forces was completed, concealed behind the houses of the city. The positioning of reserves and ammunition was started. All patches of woods behind Brobruisk were full of vehicles. They were so well camouflaged from the air that you could barely make them out when you went past them from a short distance on the ground.

The first day in Brobruisk was followed by a restless night, in which there was a constant crashing and booming in the already occupied city.

The next morning, a Sunday, looked about the same as the previous day, albeit the preparations for the crossing of the Beresina had blossomed even more in the meantime. The German artillery covered the Bolsheviks with cannon and howitzer fire. They were kept low enough that the engineers could start with the building of a new bridge over the Beresina towards evening. The enemy artillery fired only heavy shells from a great distance. The innumerable rounds were directed against the old road bridge that led over the river that had been demolished. But there was not a single German soldier to be found there.

While only a narrow strip of riverbank had been occupied on the German side up to that point, the positions along the west bank of the Beresina started to spread out. In the course of those movements, one of the *Flak* battalions, which accompanied the tanks, occupied the airstrip on the south side of the city and, in the process, captured numerous Soviet fighters and bombers.

The Bolsheviks were only able to hold up the advance to the Beresina for two days as a result of their demolished bridges and vigorous resistance. Very early in the morning of the third day, the first German rifle formations of larger size crossed over to the east bank and expanded the bridgehead that the assault detachments had already established. Fighting continuously, they worked their way through the outskirts of the city along the Beresina, a collection of wooden houses on the east bank that went up in flames in the course of the fighting that ensued. The crossing of the river, which was made all the more difficult because a tributary of the Beresina also had to be crossed, had been forced.

The Bolsheviks, who wanted to prevent the crossing of the German forces to the east bank at any cost, employed their infantry in immediate counterattacks to press the German riflemen back across the river. The

Soviet soldiers assaulted with a "Hurrah!" Bitter fighting ensued in the wet meadowlands next to the river, in the burning houses of the suburbs, and on the yellow sand along the river. The Bolshevik attack collapsed in the face of the German fires.

What the Bolsheviks could not achieve with their ground forces was then attempted from the air. Entire squadrons of Martin[1] bombers approached in waves. The bombs burst around the bridge site; *Flak* shrapnel rained down. The machine guns hammered for the east bank. The artillery of both sides continued to fire. Even an enemy armored train joined the fray, albeit without success. The fire in the suburbs continued to devour everything in sight. The riflemen received reinforcements, who ran forward through the hail of bombs and shellfire.

The fighting along the Beresina had reached its high point in the violent melee in the smallest of areas around the bridgehead. There were bloody casualties on the German side as well, but the riflemen crossing the river could not be stopped, since the enemy bombers were unable to land a single bomb on the bridge, despite all their efforts. Only the footbridge that led across the tributary of the Beresina was hit and burned down. The motorcycle infantry and the *Kübelwagen* labored through the sand along the river and found a detour through the glowing ashes of the suburbs to make it over to the east bank.

While the German attack continued to gain ground in the course of the day, wild fighting continued to take place in the air. The German fighters had one of their best days. The Bolshevik bombers crashed in flames in almost the same formations as they used to approach. Whenever the Red Stars came into contact with the ground, gigantic lances of flame shot up out of the meadowlands along the river, from the pinewoods that marked the horizon, and between the wooden houses of the residential areas. Following that, high, black clouds of smoke blew up and away at all the places where the large Martin bombers had crashed and their bombs and fuel exploded.

All of those individual columns of smoke blended together in the skies over Brobruisk into a single, gigantic, gloomy cloudbank that hung over the entire countryside and slowly blew over to the German positions, driven by the east wind. Crackling like beech wood in a chimney fire, the

---

1. Editor's Note: The Germans tended to call all Soviet twin-engine bombers "Martins" after the U.S. bomber. Most likely, these aircraft were actually SB-2s.

machine-gun ammunition burst in the black, smoke-oozing piles of rubble and kept the souvenir hunters among the *Landser* at a respectful distance. In the air, aviators dangled from their parachutes on their way to earth. Search parties in motorcycles and *Kübelwagen* raced in the direction of the shot-down aviators and took them for interrogation to the division headquarters, where the division intelligence officer and the translator assigned to him had so much ingress that they didn't know how they would handle it all.

The Soviets employed the air force along the Beresina without regard for consequences. Among their bomber crews, there were probably no more than three or four who had actually made combat sorties. Scattered by the German *Flak* and hunted down by the German fighters, the Soviets did not enjoy a long life. Only the Ratas[2], the Soviet fighters, escaped the German defenses occasionally by diving out of their hiding places in the clouds and strafing the roads in low-level flight. They then avoid an open fight—fighter versus fighter—by quickly escaping.

But the efforts of the Soviet air force to prevent the crossing of the German mechanized forces over the Beresina was pointless. By evening of the third day of fighting, the German lead elements were far forward of the east bank of the river. They organized in their well-proven march order—tanks in the lead—that they had used to advance 400 kilometers across White Russia and break all resistance.

An idea of the morale that dominated the ranks of the Soviet forces can be gleaned by the interrogation of a lieutenant who had been directed to hold up the German march column at the Ola, a small, marshy waterway in the meadowlands. The Caucasian lieutenant from a Soviet rifle regiment was taken prisoner on 2 July 1941, after his company and an adjacent one had been wiped out after a fight with German tanks in the vanguard. None of the Soviet soldiers could flee, since the bridge behind them over the marshland river had been burned down by their own people. Only the two political commissars, whom the lieutenant wanted to take prisoner and deliver to the Germans—according to his statement—had been able to escape to the rear. The Soviet officer stated that the communications network of the Soviet forces had been almost completely torn apart since the first day of the war. It often happened that one simply forgot to inform

---

2. Editor's Note: The Polikarpov I-16, the standard Soviet fighter aircraft at that time, was no match for the far more modern *Bf 109*.

troop elements that were up front of the further retreat of the Soviet army. All that was information that was already known but which was confirmed one more time.

Especially interesting, however, were the statements the Soviet officer made with regard to the war preparations of the Soviet Union. According to them, complete companies had been detached from all active Soviet regiments in the entire union for months on end to move to the western part of the Soviet Union, that is, on the edge of the German sphere of influence, to be used in constructing airstrips, field fortifications, storage facilities, wood encampments, etc. The Soviet soldiers had been informed that the day of attack against the *Reich* was 1 September 1941.

The German armed forces had therefore beaten the Soviets to the punch, and German Army formations were already marching far into White Ruthenia in the first days of July 1941 towards the Dnjepr. The Bolsheviks had two blocking positions on the way from the Beresina to the Dnjepr.

A large obstacle, which was positioned across the way of the assaulting German armored formations, the Beresina, had been crossed. Despite all their efforts, despite massed employment of artillery and bombers, the Bolsheviks had been unable to turn the tide of fate. On the east side of the river and along the course of the route of advance was the materiel that they had lost in their retreat. It was mostly tanks and antitank guns that fell into the hands of the tanks advancing at the head of the march columns as booty. A number of aircraft were also captured at an airfield that was off of the advance route.

The next march objective was the city of Rogatschew. It was there that that the armored advance route encountered the largest obstacle that inserted itself across the German route of advance, the Dnjepr. It was almost the same scene as at Brobruisk on the Beresina when the German lead elements approached Rogatschew. The enemy rearguards fought their way back through the city and across the river. The Soviet artillery fired barrage fire from the east back of the mighty river. All of the wooden bridges were ablaze. The German lead elements attempted to follow the enemy through the city and across the river, but they were unsuccessful. That was because there was a new natural obstacle that inserted itself between the pursuer and the pursued: the fifty-meter-wide tributary of the Dnjepr, the Drut, which flowed along at a sharp angle, almost parallel to the big river, before it finally emptied into it. All of the bridges leading over the Drut had also been destroyed. The city of Rogatschew was located between the two rivers like a long, narrow peninsula.

The heavy barrage fires of the enemy crashed all along the Rogatschew river sector. The black-spraying fountains of earth from the impacts were everywhere: The meadowlands, the houses and the fields. Rogatschew proper was burning from one end to the other.

To the east, in front of the German forces, which had advanced another fifty-eight kilometers in a wild assault and who again had to prepare to cross another difficult natural obstacle, there was a gloomy fire cloud that arose above the city like a sky-high wall. The Soviet commanders fired with disregard on the residents of the cities so as to buy a few more days of life in Moscow. Once again, as in Brobruisk, the eyes and ears of the German artillery arrived outside of Rogatschew with the lead German forces. They were pleased to observe every artillery round fired by the Bolsheviks, since they could determine the locations of the Bolshevik batteries by the sounds of the gun reports and the muzzle flashes.

As had been the case at the Beresina, the first hot day along the Dnjepr was followed by a storm-filled night, whose darkness was illuminated eerily by the blazing flames of burning Rogatschew and the surrounding villages. In the light of the fires, the long march columns of the German forces moving forward could be identified. Day and night, the officers and enlisted personnel have not left their vehicles since the start of the war in the East, with the exception to fight or when Soviet bombers were in the heavens. For mechanized forces, the vehicles are simultaneously a means to fight and a means to move. They are also bed and residence. The drivers, especially the motorcyclists, use every break in the march to try to catch up on lost sleep. They lay bent over across the steering wheels of their vehicles and sleep the sleep of the dead, only to be wide awake again when the column moves out and heads forward one more time.

The next morning, the German forces crossed the Drut in two strong groups and felt their way towards Rogatschew. Rifle companies, taking casualties, worked their way across the river and all the way through the burning city, in which it was crackling and crashing from one end to the other and in which shrapnel, stones, beams, boards, iron rods, roofing tiles, dirt, and dust were flying about. The riflemen crossed through that hell and advanced far enough to see the Dnjepr. They went into position along its banks with machine guns, antitank guns, and infantry guns.

A tank battalion swung out far to the north and forded the marshy Drut with its fighting vehicles, completely unnoticed by the Bolsheviks. It was a risky undertaking trying something like that with the heavy vehicles in that uncertain terrain. But the operation succeeded. The battalion reorganized on the far bank. The tank companies moved independently farther to the east. They surprised the Bolsheviks by this maneuver, much like Ziethen[3] in his day, when he approached from a side that was never expected by the enemy. A great deal of materiel, especially antitank guns, was taken in, as well as a number of prisoners. The Bolsheviks suffered considerable losses in dead and wounded. What remained of the Soviet elements scattered and disappeared into the woods. On the German side, there had been no losses since the tanks identified the antitank guns in a timely manner and eliminated them.

The German lead elements to the north of Rogatschew were thus along the Dnjepr, one of the major rivers, as well. In front of the scouts was a four-to-five-kilometer-wide stretch of broad marshy terrain, with occasional high, sandy banks on both sides, which the river snaked through. The river and its marshy bottomland were truly a considerable obstacle for an attacker, if a tough defender was behind it sufficiently armed with good weapons and enough ammunition.

For the Soviets here on the Dnjepr that was the case. The Soviet command had assembled a large force behind the river that was growing larger each day. What they could not accomplish on the Beresina is something the Soviets wanted to try again on the Dnjepr: hold up the German advance. As a result, the front ran along the river for a few days. There was intense and decisive fighting along its banks. But all of the difficulties—no matter how large and unsolvable they appeared to be— were mastered by the officers and enlisted personnel, who fought with the greatest self-sacrifice and courage, and the old, experienced commanders of *Generalleutnant* Model's division. One would talk about the hard fighting on the Dnjepr for a long time in the hometown of the division, in the garrisons of its regiments, and within the families of those who fought there.

---

3. Translator's Note: A cavalry commander under Frederick the Great.

THE HISTORY OF *PANZER-REGIMENT 6*

The regimental history[4] of *Panzer-Regiment 6* records the events of this chapter as follows:

Towards noon, continuous, intense aerial attacks from the Russian air force commenced. The enemy was attempting to prevent a crossing over the Beresina with all means at his disposal. German fighters under *Major* Mölders pounced on the bombers and fighters. The regiment bore witness to a lot of aerial fighting over its area. Every few minutes, a Russian bomber plunged earthward, burning.

In the meantime, the riflemen succeeded in establishing a small bridgehead over the Beresina. But due to the ongoing aerial attacks, the main road could barely be used by vehicles. The regiment therefore conducted reconnaissance on foot. A high-priority order from the division at 1245 hours to hurriedly move the 1st Battalion to the northern edge of the city because of a supposedly strong Russian attack across the Beresina was overcome by events, since friendly outposts had already driven the Russians—about three companies strong—back across the river. During the evening, a platoon from the 2nd Battalion was sent across the river into the small bridgehead in ferries; the bridgehead was under heavy enemy fire.

Because its commander had been wounded, the tank brigade headquarters was dissolved that day. In the future, the regiment would receive its orders directly from the division, which undoubtedly simplified the chain of command.[5] The vehicles of the armored brigade were transferred to the regiment. The rifle brigade headquarters remained.

The regiment was alerted during the night of 29–30 June. The intent of the division was to advance through Rogatschew in the direction of Mogilew. The crossing of the Beresina did not make progress, however, since the Russians were directing strong attacks against the bridgehead

---

4. Translator's Note: Munzel, *Gekämpft, gesiegt, verlosen*, 70–72.
5. Translator's Note: The armored brigades had originally been established to provide command and control for two tank regiments. Since most of the armored
   divisions no longer had two tank regiments, the command structure was largely
   superfluous. Tank brigades were formed again later in the war (1944), but they
   were separate formations with their own command-and-control structure and
   logistical support. They were a combined-arms formation with not only a tank
   battalion, but also a battalion of mechanized infantry and other combat-support
   assets, mostly company-size. They were intended as rapid-reaction forces and
   saw limited employment in late 1944 until absorbed by the armored divisions.

and the bridge was damaged over and over again. The regiment then had to send a company to support a neighboring division, which was hard pressed on the left near Swislosch. Although elements of the division succeeded in storming the locality of Titowka just north of the bridgehead, massed Russian aerial attacks there made further progress impossible. It was not until 1500 hours when the cloud cover parted that Mölder's wing and friendly *Flak* were able to respond. A dramatic battle in the air took place in front of the eyes of the regiment. More than 100 Russian aircraft were shot down and Russians who had bailed out with parachutes were taken prisoner.

The crossing could finally take place early on 1 July. The 2nd Battalion had already been taken across the previous night. Due to the large number of demolitions and the deep sandy or marshy terrain, progress was slow. The new advance guard of the division, with the 3rd Battalion in the lead, received the mission to cross the Ola. During the attempt to go around the destroyed bridge there, the tank platoon of *Leutnant* Bodig ran into an airstrip by surprise and destroyed ten enemy bombers and three Ratas. In the process, three friendly tanks were knocked out by enemy antiaircraft guns. While the riflemen of the division attempted to take the locality of Bortniki on the east bank of the river, a *Kampfgruppe* comprised of the 2nd Battalion and riflemen under the command of the regimental commander moved out at 1630 hours to swing left and cross a bridge over the Ola that was discovered intact. Once across, the *Kampfgruppe* was to move along the east bank and hit the enemy at Bortniki in the flanks and rear. But a cloudburst caused all of the wheeled vehicles to get stuck. After the motorcycle infantry mounted the tanks, it was possible to take the locality of Bortniki by a rapid thrust from the north and thus link up with the elements of the division that were advancing frontally.

At 0800 hours on 2 July, the reinforced advance guard of the 2nd Battalion moved out in the direction of Rogatschew, although it was without combat vehicles. The main body of the regiment was still held up on the advance route and suffered some casualties as a result of enemy aerial attacks. The 8th Company, which was moving in the lead, reported that it crossed the Duboschna a few kilometers outside of Rogatschew on a bridge that was badly damaged but still passable, using caution. The entire *Kampfgruppe* followed on a bridge at Filipowitschi, and the 2nd Battalion reached the railway line outside of Rogatschew at 1110 hours. But the bridge leading across the Drut there was destroyed, with the result that the attack on Rogatschew had to be initially postponed, especially since there was heavy enemy fire coming form there. During the night, the regiment received several orders while the personnel rested next to their vehicles. There was to be a different attempt to force the Dnjepr at Stary-Bychow, but impassable routes and no bridge prevented those plans. In the end, Rogatschew was taken the following afternoon against stubborn resistance by a strong attack group of the division, supported by the 3rd Battalion. During the night, the city was subjected to heavy enemy fire.

While the 1st and 2nd Battalions of the regiment received some urgently needed rest on 4 July, the riflemen succeeded in establishing a small bridgehead on the east bank of the Dnjepr at 1800 hours. Of decisive importance in doing that was the participation of three submergible tanks under *Oberfeldwebel* Blaich.[6] Although one of the vehicles was destroyed in the process, the remaining two formed the backbone of the small bridgehead. *Oberfeldwebel* Blaich later received the Knight's Cross for his actions.[7]

THE DIVISIONAL HISTORY

The divisional history[8] records the events of this chapter as follows:

General Model found himself at the edge of Brobruisk; the commander of *Schützen-Regiment 394* (*Oberstleutnant* Audörsch) arrived at the division commander's location, while the battalions of the regiment approached Brobruisk by means of detours (all of the bridges along the main road had been blown up). Reports concerning counterattacks of the Russians against the citadel arrived at the commander's location. *General* Model issued the following order to *Oberstleutnant* Audörsch at that critical moment: "Assume command of all forces in the citadel. All elements of the division that arrive are attached to you. Hold the citadel and then clear Brobruisk." That order could be executed in its entirety; all of the

---

6. Editor's Note: *Tauchpanzer III*, based on the *Panzer III*, 168 were converted in 1940. The *Tauchpanzer III* could operate at depths up to fifteen meters.

7. Translator's Note: Albert Blaich was assigned to the *12./Panzer-Regiment 6*. He was killed before war's end on 15 March 1945. It is not known why the firsthand account does not mention this aspect of the crossings, since it would have made for interesting home-front consumption. Since the submergible tank, the *Tauchpanzer III*, was surrounded with an aura of secrecy, perhaps it was not mentioned for operational security reasons.

8. Translator's Note: Traditionsverband, *Geschichte*, 119–26.

counterattacks against the citadel were turned back, meaning that the city could then start to be cleared. The forces of *Schützen-Regiment 394*, which had arrived in the meantime, were committed by company in the various city blocks to clear them. Small skirmishes ensued. But resistance was soon broken and Brobruisk was completely clear of the enemy. The lead elements of *Schützen-Regiment 394* were along the banks of the Beresina. Unfortunately, the big bridge was blown up. Since the Russians held the riverbanks under continuous fire, a hasty crossing was not possible. *Oberstleutnant* Audörsch and his command post were in the bastion right along the Beresina. The artillery had also sent its observers forward to the Beresina. They dug in behind the walls of the citadel, which were fifteen meters high right on water's edge. *Pionier-Bataillon 39* was moved into the citadel to occupy it. *Panzer-Regiment 6* arrived at the western portion of Brobruisk, and the tanks were refueled and rearmed.

The Soviets wanted to hold up the Germans at the Beresina at all costs. They brought up several batteries to the east bank and continuously shelled the city. The Soviet fire kept up the entire day, focusing on the citadel. The first officer from *Artillerie-Regiment 75* to be killed in this campaign—*Oberleutnant* Weihe, the battery commander of the 9th Battery—lost his life early in the afternoon.

All of a sudden, the skies darkened. A storm with flashing lightning, rolling thunder, and cloudbursts let loose on the river flood plain. Despite that, the Russian fire continued across the Beresina. Enemy forces used the haze of the storm to climb across the planks of the blown-up bridge. The Soviets even succeeded in reaching the German side. They were then caught by the machine guns of the *II./Schützen-Regiment 394* and had to pull back rapidly.

The division, which also moved its command post to Brobruisk in the afternoon, ordered the *II./Schützen-Regiment 394* to form a bridgehead on the east bank of the Beresina that evening. Friendly batteries initiated the operations with a preparatory fire. The riflemen made it across the river in inflatable craft; a few took the route over the destroyed bridge. The Russians put up a bitter defense. Despite that, the battalion succeeded in establishing a small bridgehead by morning. *Major* Dr. Müller was able to enter the small village of Titowka with his companies. The *2./Pionier-Bataillon 39* (*Oberleutnant* Roever) was the first to enter the village. Hard

fighting developed, during which the engineer company lost four dead
and fifteen wounded.

The engineers of the *1./Pionier-Bataillon 39* immediately started to work
on a pontoon bridge and labored the entire night. Although Russian fires
disrupted the work, it continued to make progress. For the construction
of this bridge and others, *Pionier-Bataillon 79*[9] was attached to the division.
But the river was too wide to rapidly cross large portions of the division.
The *3. Panzer-Division* extended its positions on the west bank of the river.
In the course of those movements, the airstrip south of Brobruisk was also
occupied, whereby a few machines fell undamaged into German hands.

The *II./Schützen-Regiment 394* was all by itself on the far side of the
Beresina and could only be supported by artillery that sent its fiery
greetings across the river. The brave riflemen urgently needed that help,
since they were exposed to ongoing Russian immediate counterattacks,
which focused especially on Titowka. Despite everything, *Major* Dr. Müller
was able to beat back all of the Russian attacks through his own personal
and brave example.

The *3. Panzer-Division* was held up for two days on the Beresina. It
was impossible to get across the river with larger forces. Although the
engineers were working constantly on the construction of the field-
expedient and the pontoon bridge, Russian aircraft attacked continuously,
causing casualties and adding new damage to the work in progress. The
highest command levels of the Red Army had identified the danger
associated with the German offensive in the central sector of the front
and attempted to prevent another breakthrough with all means available.
The Russian commander in chief of the Western Front was relieved and
General Jeremenko replaced him. General Jeremenko would prove to be
the main antagonist to *Generaloberst* Guderian.

The friendly *Flak* elements gave it their best, but they were too weak to
turn back all of the enemy air attacks. On 29 June, the *Flak* batteries shot
down more than twenty Soviet aircraft; on the next day, it was thirty-five.
The employment of *Oberstleutnant* Mölders's wing brought the riflemen
considerable relief. The wing shot down so many Russian machines that
soon barely any Soviet aircraft dared to show themselves on the horizon.

---

9. Translator's Note: *Panzer-Pionier-Bataillon 79* was the engineer battalion of the
   4. Panzer-Division.

Schützen-Regiment 3, which had been behind the division in the second wave up to this point, moved into Brobruisk on 29 June. At the orders conference, the division commander ordered the *I./Schützen-Regiment 3* to send a patrol to the east bank of the Beresina that very night. *Leutnant* Vormann of the 3rd Company conducted the mission and was able to determine that the Russians had apparently voluntarily evacuated their positions.

Working feverishly, *Pionier-Bataillon 39* (*Major* Beigel) was able to complete the pontoon bridge over the river during the night of 29–30 June. The division thereupon ordered that the advance was to continue the following morning. The bivouacking forces were alerted at 0600 hours and were informed to be ready to move out fifteen minutes later. But the Russians along the river did not give up and continued to place well-aimed fire on the bridge construction sites. The *II./Schützen-Regiment 394* (*Major* Dr. Müller) was all by itself on the east bank of the Beresina, and its riflemen had been constantly defending day and night the last two days. During the morning of 30 June, the battalion finally succeeded in clearing the locality of Titowka of the enemy, thus establishing a point of departure for the continued advance.

The *1./Schützen-Regiment 394* in its armored personnel carriers was the first unit to cross the finished bridge to the east bank of the river. The remaining companies of the *I./Schützen-Regiment 394* followed. The battalion immediately inserted itself into the marshlands next to the *II./ Schützen-Regiment 394* and expanded the bridgehead in all directions, one hour at a time.

Schützen-Regiment 3 (*Oberst* von Manteuffel) was brought forward to the west bank of the river from Kemenka at 1000 hours. The *II./Schützen-Regiment 3* crossed the Beresina from the northern portion of Brobruisk. The *I./Schützen-Regiment 3* crossed the water obstacle on the pontoon bridge. Crossing the river south of the city in inflatable craft was the *3./ Schützen-Regiment 3*. That company encountered heavy defensive fire in front of the railway embankment and suffered three dead and several wounded. Both of the regiments were on the east bank and drove wedges into the enemy front. Finally, the Russians turned tail and pulled back through the marshy flood plain to the east. The only thing that continued to be active was the Soviet air force, which attacked the crossing point in waves.

The continuing bomber attacks were also the reason why the tank regiment did not cross the river that day. Towards noon, the two battalions moved back to their bivouac areas west of Brobruisk, although their orders to be prepared to move continued to be in effect. An exception was a platoon of the *2./Panzer-Regiment 6* under *Leutnant* von Wedel, which was attached to *Aufklärungs-Abteilung 1* to form an advance guard. Around 1600 hours in the afternoon, the brigade provided the following situation report: "Movement east stopped. For the rest of the day, rest and maintenance." A few hours later, the armored brigade headquarters was dissolved. That meant that the armored brigade of the *3. Panzer-Division* had ceased to exist. The command vehicles of the headquarters were issued to *Oberstleutnant* von Lewinski, and he was placed under the direct command and control of the division.

During the day, the two rifle regiments expanded their bridgeheads. Towards 1900 hours, *Schützen-Regiment 3* reached Babin, seven kilometers east of the Beresina. At that point, the *II./Schützen-Regiment 3* and the *II./Schützen-Regiment 394* were north of the main avenue of advance, while the two other battalions were to the south of it. Forward of Babin, the *I./Schützen-Regiment 3* screened to the southeast. The Soviets continued to try to turn back the regiments by means of air attacks, but their efforts were fruitless.

The *3. Panzer-Division* went across the military bridges to the east bank of the Beresina with its remaining elements. Starting at 0600 hours, *Panzer-Regiment 6* formed up to move through Brobruisk and started crossing the river three quarters of an hour later with its lead elements. Since the flood bridges had been blown up on the far side, long stretches of detour had to be driven through deep sand. The wheeled vehicles could only make it hooked up to tanks in front of them. After moving through the badly damaged Totowka, the tank regiment bivouacked in the woods near Babin.

The division had ordered its attack in the direction of Rogatschew. A strong advance guard under *Oberst* Kleemann was established for that purpose. *Panzer-Regiment 6* detached its 3rd Battalion (*Hauptmann* Schneider-Kostalski), while *Schützen-Regiment 3* detached a mixed company under the command of *Oberleutnant* von Baumbach. The first mission for the advance guard: locate the enemy and determine his strength; determine which bridges are destroyed; take intact bridges.

The advance guard moved out at 1030 hours. The tanks, armored personnel carriers, and motorcycles made good progress until they reached Ola Creek, and a destroyed bridge there prevented their further movement. *Leutnant* Bodig's tank platoon was given the mission of reconnoitering for a detour as part of *Oberleutnant* Baumbach's mixed company. In the process, the fighting vehicles were surprised to find an enemy airfield. Both sides were equally surprised. German tanks and Russian antiaircraft weapons opened fire at the same time. Three friendly tanks and one armored personnel carrier were knocked out and set alight. In the end, however, the enemy resistance was broken. Three Rata fighters and ten bombers were destroyed on the ground. *Leutnant* Haug was sent back by the commander of the advance guard to render a report. He encountered the rifle brigade 5.5 kilometers east of Babin, where a blown-up bridge was holding up its advance. A short while later, *Oberleutnant* von Baumbach returned with his company after successfully completing his mission.

Generalleutnant Model personally moved forward to breathe some life into the advance, which had bogged down. In the meantime, *Aufklärungs-Abteilung 1* (*Hauptmann* Ziervogel) had discovered an intact bridge at Pawlowitschi. At that point, *Generalleutnant* Model issued new orders. According to them, *Oberstleutnant* von Lewinski was to swing out with his 2nd Battalion to the left once across the bridge and reach the road again to the rear of the enemy. The rifle brigade was to advance on both sides of the road in two assault groups and go around the Russian position at the destroyed bridge.

A cloudburst commenced at the same time that the tanks and the riflemen started out. For the most part, the wheeled vehicles got stuck in the mud. *Oberstleutnant* Munzel thereupon had the riflemen of the *II./ Schützen-Regiment 3* mount his tanks, while the *I./Schützen-Regiment 3* had to fight its way with difficulty through the marsh and mud. The *5./Panzer-Regiment 6* advanced directly east, while the remaining elements of the regiment pressed south from the far bank of the Ola. The *I./Schützen-Regiment 3* (*Major* Wellmann), supported by elements from *Pionier-Bataillon 39*, crossed in rafts and drove the Russians in front of it away. The riflemen linked up with the tankers of *Panzer-Regiment 6* at Bortniki. Towards 2300 hours, *Schützen-Regiment 3* transitioned to screening around Bortniki. The

II./Schützen-Regiment 3 (*Major* Zimmermann) was to the left of the road, the 1st Battalion to the right.

The morning of 2 July promised another day of warm weather. *Panzer-Regiment 6* was awakened shortly after 0500 hours. *Oberstleutnant* von Lewinski only had the *II./Panzer-Regiment 6* at his disposal at the time, since the combat trains of the 1st Battalion had not made it forward yet and the battalion needed to be refueled and rearmed. The *II./Panzer-Regiment 6* moved out at 0805 hours. The point was formed this time by the *8./Panzer-Regiment 6*. The company made rapid progress, but it was unable to cross the Dubysna, since the bridge had been blown up by the enemy at Liskowskaja. The fighting vehicles were able to discover a bridge capable of taking tanks to the north at Filipkowitschi. *Oberstleutnant* Munzel moved his entire battalion there, crossing the small river.

The remaining elements of the battalion followed slowly. Russian aircraft repeatedly attacked the columns in the morning. A short while later, fifteen close-support aircraft came in, followed by eight fighters. The aircraft flew at low level over the battalions and strafed, causing casualties and damage to the vehicles.

Most of the division was still bogged down in front of the Dubysna. The bridging columns of *Pionier-Bataillon 39* were employed and built a sixteen-ton bridge. The construction did not proceed as quickly as expected, since enemy aircraft continuously forced the engineers to seek cover. It was not until around 1900 hours that the work was completed; at that point, the vehicles started rolling again. In the meantime, the *3. Panzer-Division* had issued orders for the next day. The advance guard under *Oberstleutnant* Munzel advanced as far as the rail line in front of Rogatschew with its lead elements towards 1100 hours. One half hour later, it reported by radio: "Bridge over the Drut in front of Rogatschew blown up. Correspondingly impossible to advance at this time. Enemy artillery fire." At that point, *Generalleutnant* Model issued orders for a halt. *Panzer-Regiment 6* pulled off of the road and set up security in the area around Trotzky. Smaller elements remained screening along the Drut.

The *3. Panzer-Division* had thus reached the largest natural obstacle so far in its advance. The fifty-meter-wide Drut separated the regiments from the enemy side. That was followed by the marshy flood plains of the Dnjepr. The city of Rogatschew was located in the sharp corner of the confluence of the two rivers and dominated the entire region. The city was already burning. The *II./Schützen-Regiment 3* of *Major* Zimmermann, reinforced by engineers and a platoon of antitank guns, attacked Rogatschew in a *coup de main*. The riflemen, some of them mounted on the antitank vehicles, assaulted along the narrow road. The resistance offered by individual machine-gun nests was rapidly broken. They reached the high ground west of the city, where they saw the enemy blow up the bridges. That meant that the objective could no longer be obtained. *Major* Zimmermann issued orders to set up a hedgehog defense on the high ground. Fortunately, the milk processing plant—a fairly modern installation—remained in the hands of the riflemen, who were able to indulge in milk and cheese, before nightfall descended.

The *3. Panzer-Division* closed up to the river in the evening and during the night. Enemy artillery fire repeatedly disrupted friendly movements. Three large bomb craters temporarily rendered the main road useless. Patrols and route reconnaissance elements that were sent out determined that the Liskowskaja–Bartschiza–Tschgirink road, which was needed for an advance on Star-Bychow, was completely impassable to wheeled vehicles. That meant that an attack to the northeast was out of the question for the time being.

The division command therefore decided to attack Rogatschew frontally, in order to eliminate this "fire-spewing" Russian city and strongpoint and create a bridgehead to the east bank of the Dnjepr. The *III./Schützen-Regiment 3* (*Major* Zimmermann), the *I./Schützen-Regiment 394* (*Hauptmann* Pape) and the *III./Panzer-Regiment 6* (*Hauptmann* Schneider-Kostalski) were employed to that end. In addition, there were elements from *Panzerjäger-Abteilung 543* (*Major Freiherr* von Türckheim), *Pionier-Bataillon 39* (*Major* Beigel), and the *II./Schützen-Regiment 394* (*Major Dr.* Müller). *Oberst* Ries's *Artillerie-Regiment 75*, which had closed up, started preparatory fires on burning Rogatschew and Russian positions on both sides of the river at 1800 hours on that Thursday, 3 July. The Russian artillery did not remain silent, either. It placed harassing fires all across the sector, especially along the bridge on the railway embankment.

The *III./Panzer-Regiment 6*, together with the *I./Schützen-Regiment 394*, approached the Drut through its green, vegetated flood plains, winding its way through the marshy meadows. Numerous wooden rafts were in the water, which was not deep. The *9./Panzer-Regiment 6* of *Hauptmann* Streger initially approached the river. The tanks buttoned up. The fighting vehicles rattled into the shallow and marshy waters. The remaining companies waited a few minutes to see what happened to the fording company. When the first tank climbed out of the Drut on the far bank, *Hauptmann* Schneider-Kostalski issued orders: *"Panzer marsch!"* The entire battalion was able to get through the river without incident. The riflemen followed closely behind and, in some instances, used the wooden rafts to cross. Despite suborn defensive fires, the tanks and the riflemen were in front of the burning wooden huts on the northern edge of Rogatschew a short while later.

At the same time, the *II./Schützen-Regiment 3*, the *II./Schützen-Regiment 394*, and the *3./Pionier-Bataillon 39* moved out to attack the city. The two battalions moved into Rogatschew fairly rapidly. The riflemen and engineers fought their way in, meter by meter. Murderous fire was received from all of the houses. The Russians defended desperately. The antitank gun crews pushed and pulled their guns by hand and individually took the pockets of resistance under fire.

The houses and the roads were burning everywhere. The battalions slowly chewed their way into the city. The platoon of *Leutnant* Möllhoff (*3./Pionier-Bataillon 39*) reached the church in the center of the city. Then the riflemen were at the Dnjepr. Extremely heavy machine-gun and artillery fire was received from the far bank, forcing the riflemen to take cover. *Oberstleutnant* Audörsch (commander of *Schützen-Regiment 394*) and *Major* Zimmermann (commander of *Schützen-Regiment 3*) were in the city and discussed how to conduct the fight there as well as a possible crossing of the Dnjepr. During the night, during which the enemy artillery fire had not slowed down at all, one of the division chaplains, Dr. Heiland, made a surprise visit to the command post of *Schützen-Regiment 394*. As he had done so frequently before, he had come forward to the forward lines to care for the wounded. For his constant presence among the lead elements and his unflappability, he was awarded the Iron Cross, First Class, that day.

It was only outside of Rogatschew that a few *Kampfgruppen* (the *7.* And *8./Schützen-Regiment 3*) were able to get across the river. From the *6./Schützen-Regiment 3*, only *Leutnant* Saathoff made it across the water. The engineers made another crossing attempt, until they were torn apart in the maelstrom of the hard fighting along the banks.

The fighting to establish a bridgehead at Rogatschew started. Since the Soviets were still defending in the city proper, our soldiers quickly got into a difficult situation. The losses mounted from hour to hour. *Oberleutnant* Spillmann, the company commander of the *6./Schützen-Regiment 394*, fell along with many of his soldiers. *Major* Zimmermann, the commander of the *II./Schützen-Regiment 3*, was wounded for the third time. *Hauptmann* Engelien assumed acting command of the battalion. The *8./Schützen-Regiment 3*, which had been employed as a flank guard in the direction of Salutje, took the heaviest casualties. The company commander, *Oberleutnant* Becker, was badly wounded; *Leutnant* Fritze was killed. *Leutnant* Gleitz, the leader of an engineer assault detachment, was mortally wounded, along with three other enlisted engineer personnel. At that point, the acting commander of the *3./Pionier-Bataillon 39*, *Leutnant* Schultze, assumed command of all surviving forces in the bridgehead and ordered a withdrawal across the river.

While the fighting vehicles of the *III./Panzer-Regiment 6* pulled back to the city's edge during the night, the riflemen remained in contact with the enemy. He was putting up particularly stiff resistance in the southern part of the city. For the time being, there was no progress. The rifle brigade issued orders that the *I./Schützen-Regiment 3*, which had not yet been committed, reinforce the outposts in that area with some of its elements. The *1./Schützen-Regiment 3* of *Oberleutnant* von Ztizewitz was reinforced with platoons from the 2nd, 4th, and 5th Companies, as well as a platoon from *Panzerjäger-Abteilung 543*, and given that mission. The reinforced company received its designated sector shortly after 2100 hours and dug in among the vegetated terrain southwest of the railway bridge.

The morning of 4 July saw no change to the situation. The fighting was primarily marked on both sides by the artillery duel. The Soviets had thirty-six heavy batteries on the east bank of the Dnjepr southeast of Rogatschew, which they used to shower the German movements in and around the city with heavy fire (15 centimeter). Despite the fact that forward observers had been brought as far forward as the river, the artillery was unable to successfully engage those enemy batteries.

The numbers of wounded climbed day by day, hour by hour. The wounded, who could not be cared for at the forward clearing station, had to be transported by ambulance to the field hospital at Brobruisk, forty-two kilometers away. *Leutnant* Schickerling, the platoon leader of the 1st Ambulance Platoon, saved a wounded man by swimming across the Dnjepr. For his actions, he was later awarded the Iron Cross, First Class.

Towards noon, the rifle brigade ordered the attack of the *I./Schützen-Regiment 3*, reinforced by a platoon of tanks and two antitank companies, on Lutschin. *Major* Wellmann moved out ahead with the tanks and the *2./Schützen-Regiment 3*, who had climbed aboard, and occupied it. Once there, the riflemen linked up with *Leutnant* Stegmann and his demolition party from the *5./Schützen-Regiment 3*, which had blown up the railway facilities south of the village.

The division started to form its first bridgehead on the Dnjepr at 1800 hours. A *Stuka* attack on enemy positions had already taken place at 1500 hours, but it did not succeed in silencing the enemy artillery. The *II./Schützen-Regiment 3* attacked directly from Rogatschew, in order to establish a bridgehead. It was directed for the *II./Schützen-Regiment 394*, supported by elements of the *III./Panzer-Regiment 6*, to form a bridgehead to the north, so as to then hit the enemy in the rear, while the reinforced *3./Schützen-Regiment 3* tied down Soviet forces from the front at the Jedolin collective farm. Unfortunately, the operation stood under an unlucky star. The attack of the *II./Schützen-Regiment 3* bogged down at the city's edges. On his own initiative, *Hauptmann* Engelien called off the attack of his battalion. In the last few days, the battalion had lost all its 8th Company and an additional 146 men of the other four companies. Likewise, the attack of the *3./Schützen-Regiment 3* (*Hauptmann* Peschke) was delayed. The company was unable to attack until 2000 hours, because the inflatable rafts were brought forward too late. The company's efforts then bogged down in the face of the Russian artillery. The company thereupon dug in along the Dnjepr and had to defend against the enemy's immediate counterattacks, which were directed at Lutschkin.

The *II./Schützen-Regiment 394* (*Major* Dr. Müller) had more success. The battalion, reinforced by antitank elements, was actually able to cross the 100-meter-wide river. The three submergible tanks of the *12./Panzer-Regiment 6* (under *Oberfeldwebel* Blaich) provided powerful support to the riflemen. The tanks crossed the river under the water surface and got to the far shore. Although one of the fighting vehicles was knocked out by Russian antitank guns, the remaining two tanks held down the Russian defenses long enough for the riflemen to cross. The *6./Schützen-Regiment 394* (*Leutnant* Gappel) attacked and reached the ridgeline 100 meters east of Sborowo.

At that point, *Major* Dr. Müller was at Sborowo on the east bank of the broad river with his battalion and the *1.* and *3./Panzerjäger-Abteilung 543 (Oberleutnants* Michels and Held). That signaled the heroic struggle of those forces, which were soon cut off from the remaining elements of the division. The Soviets placed such heavy artillery fire on the riverbanks and the destroyed bridges that not a single additional man was able to cross the Dnjepr. At the same time, Russian infantry charged the positions of the small bridgehead. Casualties mounted by the hour on the German side, and rations and ammunition were slowly running out. But the few companies held firm against all attacks. The riflemen and antitank gunners knew neither sleep nor rest nor relief over the next few days. *Major* Dr. Müller compelled his men to hold out through his personal bravery. Later on, he and *Oberfeldwebel* Blaich received the Knight's Cross for their bold actions.

The *XXIV. Armee-Korps (mot.)* radioed orders during the morning that the division was not to move anymore forces into the bridgehead for the time being. In the meantime, the Drut flood plains had been made trafficable by the construction of a 1.8-kilometer-long corduroy road by the *1.* and *2./Pionier-Bataillon 39* under *Hauptmann* Winkler. The elements of the rifle regiments that had been employed were to remain in place, while *Panzer-Regiment 6* was to be prepared to support the *4. Panzer-Division.* But even those orders were changed. The movements of *Panzer-Regiment 6*, which had already been initiated, were stopped. Its 1st Battalion was attached to the *10. Infanterie-Division (mot.)* in Bortniki towards noon. *Major* Schmidt-Ott immediately headed in that direction and set up in Kaschary. The *II./Panzer-Regiment 6* remained on alert, since strong enemy movements were detected along the southern flank of the division, where *Kradschützen-Bataillon 3* was screening. A platoon from the *8./Panzer-Regiment 6* was sent towards Schlobin to reconnoiter and reported motorized Russian forces. *Leutnant* Jacobs and his light platoon from the regimental headquarters reconnoitered the area between the Drut and the Dnjepr.

The overall situation that day remained unchanged. The morning was strangely quiet; it was not until the afternoon that the enemy's artillery fires increased. The division feared large-scale enemy attacks and pulled back some of the rifle companies that had been employed to screen as reserves. Only the *II./Schützen-Regiment 394* remained in place, involved in heavy fighting in its bridgehead position. The riflemen there had been fighting for two days without letup. It was not until 6 July that the *I./ Schützen-Regiment 394* was able to cross the Dnjepr—after its companies had crossed the Drut on floating beams—and support its hard-pressed sister battalion. The casualties continued to increase, however. *Stabsarzt* Dr. Marr died after being hit in the chest as he helped transport wounded to the rear along with *Feldwebel* Feldebert. The forward observer of the *7./ Artillerie-Regiment 75*, *Leutnant* Schwendendieck, was mortally wounded at his observation post. The acting commander of the *6./Schützen-Regiment 394*, *Leutnant* Gappel, had to turn over his company to *Hauptfeldwebel* Holst after being wounded by shrapnel. Holst himself was badly wounded a short while later. *Leutnant* Rosemeyer and *Leutnant* Steinmüller were likewise badly wounded. Despite all the casualties, *Schützen-Regiment 394* continued to hold. The artillery, which was being directed by the wounded *Leutnant Graf* Studnitz, provided valuable support.

After the intoxicating successes of the first few days of war, no one had thought that the Russians would be able to pull themselves together to offer such hard resistance, even though the Dnjepr was on the so-called "Stalin Line." It was certain, however, that the *3. Panzer-Division* could not force a crossing over the Dnjepr. The corps considered sending the *4. Panzer-Division* and the *10. Infanterie-Division (mot.)* north to attack there, in order to land to the rear of the enemy, who was being held down along the front by the *3. Panzer-Division.*

On the road to Kobryn.

An observation post.

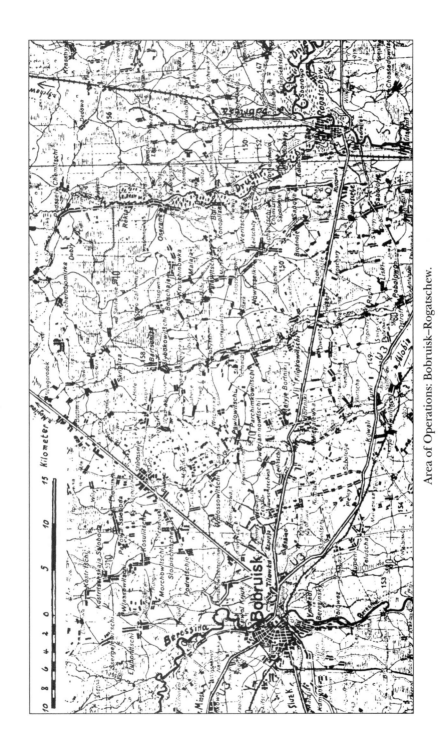

Area of Operations: Bobruisk–Rogatschew.

CHAPTER 8

Fighting for the Dnjepr Crossings

ACROSS THE DRUT INTO BURNING ROGATSCHEW

A gigantic blue-black cloud stood in the east like a signal of destruction. It was a guidepost to the front, visible from afar. It was the mushroom of smoke, undulating and billowing, from the burning city of Rogatschew. The Bolsheviks had set the city on the Dnjepr ablaze through their fires.

The fight for the decisive crossing point over the Dnjepr had erupted in all of its harshness. The armored division, as the sharp, steel wedge of our armored corps, had thrust farther into the Soviet army. On the eleventh day of the campaign, the city of Rogatschew along the Brest-Litowsk–Moscow route of advance had been reached. It is located in a large bend in the river, which is formed here by the broad Dnjepr and its tributary, the Drut. Russia's waterways—interconnected by means of numerous tributaries, with uncontrolled riverbeds run to seed, in the middle of broad, usually overflowing flood plains—from difficult-to-take fortresses whenever the bridges over the few roads are destroyed. The wildly twisting Dnjepr—after the Volga and the Danube, the third largest river in Europe—is a defensive line that is especially favored by nature. It flows straight in a north-south line through the eastern part of White Ruthenia, before it empties into the Black Sea as the main river of the Ukraine. With its tributaries, it formed the strongest obstacle for our armored corps outside of the entrance into the interior of the Soviet Republic, central Russia.

For that reason, the Bolsheviks established strong forces on the east bank to defend, as the German command had expected. About two divisions with corps artillery, as confirmed by friendly reconnaissance and the statements of prisoners and deserters. The woods to either side of the main road from Rogatschew are the focal point of the enemy resistance. They were riddled with batteries. The infantry regiments of the Soviets had set up in improved field positions. The enemy was attempting to defend

111

the Dnjepr line with all the means at his disposal. He had been introducing
reinforcements in a deliberate manner for ten days. He had attempted to
hold up the German advance by means of systematically destroying bridges.
All of the bridges over the Beresina, the historic tributary of the Dnjepr,
had been blown up or burnt down when the forward elements of the
division pressed into the citadel of Brobruisk on 28 June.

The bridges over the small tributaries of the Ola and the Dobysna had
also been destroyed. The Bolsheviks attempted to offer resistance along
the east banks there as well. It was in vain. Tanks and riflemen chased the
enemy into Rogatschew proper. On 2 July, the second bridge over the
backwaters of the Beresina had been completed. On the same day, the
attack on Rogatschew started.

Once again, the air was filled with the raging noise of roaring guns
and the sharp crack of exploding shells. It was Thursday, 3 July. The clock
showed it was exactly 0600 hours. It was the designated time for the attack
of the riflemen, the engineers and the antitank elements. The German
artillery suddenly increased its tempo. The quick succession of booming
reports sounded like powerful hammer blows on a steel anvil. The rounds
screamed high above us, gurgling and howling. Then there was an eerie
hissing and rushing noise. Like rockets, innumerable high-explosive
rounds were slung all at once onto the enemy positions. The long trails of
smoke were visible in the heavens for minutes. They had barely had time
to sink down when the howling hissing climbed once again . . . and again!
An exciting close-up of the battle. If only to be one of the fighters at this
point that take their turns around the torch smoke and fly their covering
sorties over the Dnjepr! At that moment, they were witnesses to the effects
of that destructive shower of shells.

The Bolshevik artillery replied. It arbitrarily scattered its shells into the
slightly rolling field next to the advance route. The main objective was the
road bridge above the railway line. There, you had to make short jumps
from one covered position to the next. Soldiers cowered in hastily dug-out
holes, pressed against the sandy walls. Our route led to the high, round
water tower of a dairy processing plant; it was the focal point of the entire
surrounding terrain, like a gigantic chimney. Howitzer batteries had set
up observation posts in it. A wooden stairway led to the top. There were
windows on each level, all facing the enemy. The observers were standing
on chairs. The radio operators and personnel relaying the fire missions were

sitting everywhere on the stairs with their radio sets. The hurricane of fire on the far side of the Dnjepr was directed from here. "Florian" called his guns into position so as to direct the rounds onto newly identified targets.

The red tower ended with a wide deck going all the way around it. With its many windows, it was an excellent observation deck. The battery commander was sitting at the scissor scope. The view extended far beyond Rogatschew. As far as the woods on the far side of the Dnjepr, where the muzzle flashes of the enemy guns could be seen blazing. Likewise, the Soviet observation posts had the water tower in the crosshairs of their scissor scopes. Understandably, towers that dominate the terrain such as that one were a thorn in the eye of every artilleryman. For that reason, the Bolsheviks fired again and again in the direction of the tower with a dogged passion and perseverance. Probably more than a 1,000 rounds, the *Hauptmann* opined. Given the long distance, however, hitting the target was like finding a needle in a large field. The rounds swept past. Or they landed too short and exploded in the plant facilities below us. Some of the roof trusses were already in bright flames. The slates were flying from the storage buildings. It was only on two occasions that a garish curtain of flame ripped past our observation window, causing us to quickly duck our heads. It was likely that the two rounds had slightly grazed the thick walls of the tower.

From up above you, it was impressive to see how open the land was—kilometers on end—through which the tanks and the rifle regiments had to fight. The Drut wound its way through green meadows to the Dnjepr, whose course shimmered up to us off to the right through the rows of vegetation. Of course, the wooden road bridge was destroyed. Heavy artillery fire was being placed on the road and the crossing point. A direct hit registered in the middle of the destroyed structure. Beams and boards twirled from out of the cloud formed by the explosion. The Soviets were firing with heavy calibers, most likely 15-centimeter. Behind the marshy Drut meadows was the broad expanse of the town of Rogatschew in the fork between the rivers. It was burning form one end to the other. Ten large fires were quickly swallowing up everything around them and crawling towards one another. We saw houses and villages burn down, and we raced with our vehicle through the sea of flames that was Sluzk. This city of Rogatschew, extended idyllically along a small rise in the middle of the large green expanse, is an especially shocking funeral pyre of the Bolsheviks. The wind drove the flames. The old wood of the houses burned as if it had been doused with gasoline. The frameworks of the houses were eerily visible through the brilliant red of the heat, until they finally collapsed.

Tanks, riflemen, and antitank elements were assaulting into this city, which was already burning in many places. Waterways like the Drut were no longer an obstacle for our fighting vehicles. Firing to all sides, the tanks moved across the wet meadows to the river and through the relatively shallow water to the other bank. With the start of the attack at 0600 hours, they penetrated into the northern portion of the city. A rifle battalion attacked frontally. The assault soldiers fought their way into Rogatschew in bitter street fighting, meter by meter. Murderous fires from the defenders lashed out at them from the houses. The field-gray soldiers fought with death-defying courage and self-sacrifice. They took casualties. The Bolshevik artillery fired among them. The antitank gunners man-handled their cannon forward. The heat was unbearable along many of the streets. The battalion literally chewed its way through the city. On the other side, the Dnjepr was flowing.

The blue-gray woods on the other side appeared distinctly in the scissor scopes. Fog was already hanging over the trees. Looking like a gun-sight notch, a clearing appeared off to the right. There was a constant flashing there. The observations had made out the muzzle flashes of a minimum of four batteries in that patch of woods. Several batteries had also been detected north of the road. They were still just within range of the German howitzers. On the roads leading in from Brobruisk, heavy artillery, howitzers, and powerful long-range cannon were rolling forward. The first ones would go into position that evening. The battery commander told us that the Bolsheviks had employed an armored train twice. It was armed with artillery pieces and machine guns. It had suddenly approached along the railway line that was a couple of hundred meters from the tower below the main road the previous day. The firing positions of the batteries had to be moved back 600 meters. This morning, at 0500 hours, the armored monster attempted another attack. When faced by the shells of the artillery and the antitank guns, it quickly steamed back to Shlobin, the next locality along the railway line.

The armored division had its command post in a small village next to the main road. The wells to the right and the left of the road with their tall drawing beams reminded us that Russia was a land of steppes. Just poor, miserable one-story houses. You couldn't stay inside. Bolshevism had not left enough for the populace to eat. One village looked as decrepit as the next. Correspondingly, you slept wrapped up in a blanket under shelter halves in the open. We were awakened a bit after midnight. A Soviet night bomber flew low past the locality. Its silhouette identified it as having four engines. Long flashes of fire suddenly and thunderously illuminated the night. But its stick of bombs only fell without effect in an open field.

That afternoon, the attack pressure was increased. The heavy artillery lifted its powerful bass. Right at 1500 hours, a powerful preparation was fired. A heavy load hissed over us like an aircraft engine at full throttle. The heavy long-range guns began to register. The target, over which the German reconnaissance aircraft was circling, was the railway station of the important transportation hub of Shlobin, south of Rogatschew. It was full of freight trains, as was revealed by the reconnaissance flights. An armored train and railway guns were also identified. The first reports were soon submitted by the pilot. The rounds were direct hits right in the freight yard; railway cars were already burning. Everything was racing around madly. More and more rounds were racing that way with powerful drumbeats. An extraordinary thought—to be firing in the middle of a train station of a large city from such a great distance.

At 1500 hours, the expected *Stukas* also arrived. The frequently seen sight—one that filled the German soldier with enthusiasm—was repeated along the Dnjepr. Everyone strained their necks whenever the wild hawks descended out of the light clouds, this time on the positions of the enemy infantry and the artillery in the woods. The *Ju 88's* followed, the large bombers capable of both horizontal and dive sorties. In comparison to them, the Messerschmitt fighters hunting around them came off as almost playful. The large machines approached the targets twice. Immediately after the first bomb run, the report came in to the command post from the pilots that the Bolshevik infantry was fleeing from its trenches in droves. A couple of dark, exploding clouds appeared black in the bright skies. That meant the enemy also had antiaircraft guns in position.

Antitank elements moved forward on the road at a fast pace. The heavy engineer vehicles—loaded down with pontoons and, in between, assault craft—were brought forward to the Drut. At regular intervals, fountains of earth sprang along the bridge over the railway line. A long-range Soviet gun had zeroed in on that location.

Three hours later, a new *Stuka* squadron dove down on the woods on the other side. That was the sign for the German artillery to increase its fires to hurricane strength once more. The batteries were positioned one behind the other on both sides of the road, well camouflaged from the air. In the small, vegetated areas populated by pines and birches, there were brilliant muzzle flashes everywhere. A multi-voiced chorus of rounds raced across the Drut and the Dnjepr once again. The division commander observed from the forward command post. The main attack had not yet started. Large assault detachments were employed—handpicked assault soldiers from one of the rifle regiments—that were directed across the Dnjepr. The enemy artillery responded again. Its strength was supposed to be determined after the *Stuka* attack. That had been done. The general moved back. The various commanders had assembled along the narrow village street. The orders for the next attack were issued.

The city of Rogatschew was in ruins. It was only at its outside edges that a few buildings were intact. But the name of Rogatschew will always be connected to a page of honor for one of our rifle regiments from the province of Brandenburg. Once again, the death-defying infantrymen proved they knew how to attack, how to claim victory, and how to die. Among the wounded was the battalion commander with the Knight's Cross. Shot in the arm. After Poland and France, for the third time here in Russia. His young comrades told war stories about their experiences from the campaigns; they showed how close the bonds were between the commander and his men. The irrepressible humor, which had never left him in any situation, seemed to come from an inexhaustible source. At one point, an excited messenger came calling: "*Herr Major*, artillery is firing here!"

"We know that!" he answered in his broad Berlin accent. "What do you think they're doing, showering us with candy?"

That raised everyone's spirits.

Then they talked about the comrades who had assaulted with them for the last time. Calmly and somewhat quietly, as is the soldier's way after difficult days.

The riflemen had to dig in to the south of the main road. For the time being, there was no advancing to be done there. The enemy artillery was too strong and too destructive.

To the north of the wide main road at Rogatschew, the Dnjepr makes a big curve. The small village of Sborowo was on the far bank, a locality as wretched as the rest. The history of this war gave it a special meaning. It was there that an assault detachment from the other rifle regiment of the division crossed the Dnjepr in inflatable craft and took the opposite bank. Platoons and companies followed up. Heavy infantry weapons were brought across on ferries. A strong bridgehead could be established. In raging counterattacks, Bolshevik infantry attempted to throw our people back across the Dnjepr. They worked their way along the Dnjepr along the flanks, but their attacks bogged down in the defensive fires of the defenders, despite their superior numbers. The Bolshevik artillery placed heavy fire on the village and the positions in front of it. But the riflemen clawed their way in and held on stubbornly. The German bridgehead on the Dnjepr held.

We went into the positions with the division commander. It was a route that only allowed tracked vehicles, heavy trucks with dual axles, and *Kübelwagen* to move forward.

It was part of the general's daily routine to visit the positions. That was the way it was on all fronts. But it was also understandable why the individual soldier was always happy when he saw "his" general up front with him. In a comradely way, *Generalleutnant* Model asked officers and men about their missions. He had the men give him detailed combat reports and listened concerning the difficulty of the fighting and the casualties. He knew what the men were thinking, who were lying in the muck and wetness of the Drut and the Dnjepr. But the soldiers were also happy to be able to give the division commander their input and answer his questions. Conferences with the commanders at the command post. The 3rd Company of the antitank battalion had taken casualties in Rogatschew. The general ordered that only two men were to stay with the guns, while the others remained under cover until relieved. The newly evaluated aerial reconnaissance photographs were discussed with the commander of the rifle brigade. A fighting division has to be looked after and cared for. Above all, the rations system has to function. The general devoted his attention to that as well.

It was at that spot between the Drut and the Dnjepr that the logistics lines of communication were especially difficult. There was no road. The only route available led through marsh, morass, waterways, and the rising Drut. Three small bridges led to the sixteen-ton bridge over the Drut. The earth was black and soft. The sliding foot sank deep with every step. In the meantime, there had been several downpours. The waters had risen. Where there had been firm land the previous day, there were gigantic, deep pools of water. The *Flak* positions had turned into small islands. A 1,200-meter-long corduroy road had to be constructed out of thick trunks. Several companies worked for twenty-four hours at a stretch. The one-way traffic could only move very slowly there. And the water continued to rise. New trunks and layers of wood had to be put down. The trunks were as slippery as soap. It was an art form to balance on top of them. That was the "road" to the rifle regiment employed ahead and the combat zone of our armored division. If you hadn't seen it, you couldn't have imagined it. Rations runners moved with their heavy mess cans and sacks of rations in front of us. Prisoners approached us with German wounded on stretchers. The doctors wanted to spare them being shaken up on the corduroy road. The general talked to a few of the wounded. Despite their wounds, they were in good spirits. Most of the wounds were from artillery shrapnel. The enemy artillery was hammering the bridgehead on the Dnjepr ceaselessly.

The German artillery had also gone into position along this route, a large help for the infantry. Just as we reached the embankment in front of the Dnjepr, final protective fires were requested. The howitzers fired smoke rounds from well-camouflaged positions. Milky billowing smoke rose from the woods. Signal flares went up. A couple of houses burned. The ferry was undamaged. The impacts from the enemy artillery went far astray. The banks sloped steeply. The main arm of the Dnjepr was only eighty meters wide at this spot. But the tributaries behind it were numerous. Three tanks had forded there, heartily welcomed by the infantry. The commander of the rifle regiment briefed the general. The fighting had been difficult. That was all too understandable based on the constant attacks by the Bolsheviks. Additional guns began to fire. German artillery registered for the nighttime protective fires. The last enemy attack had collapsed in the face of their fires. New attacks were expected for the coming night. The general took his leave with a hearty handshake, the mark of his obligation to the men. Sborowo is the name around which the laurels are wrapped for our other rifle regiment.

Our Brandenburg tank regiment has been fighting ever since Brest-Litowsk. It has truly been the steel tip, which has smashed into the Red front for our armored corps. It was one battalion after the other—charging ahead of the division—that had roared into the enemy's tanks and artillery. The success and the spoils of war for the armored corps through 2 July numbered 244 tanks and 199 guns. Those numbers reflect a large amount of kills that our tank regiment had made. Fighting in the last two weeks, it covered 460 kilometers, the distance from Berlin to Danzig. Now, bivouacked in the small villages in the vicinity of Rogatschew, it was time for it to get its fill of sleep.

It was the night of 5–6 July, heading into Sunday. Everyone was asleep, only the double walking guards made their rounds. The woods on either side of the main road still could not be trusted. A liaison officer swept up to the commander. Alert! It was 0500 hours. Fifteen minutes later, the first tanks rumbled off.

A Bolshevik infantry division was attempting to thrust into the flanks and rear of our armored division by advancing from the transportation hub of Shlobin. What with the long thrusts along the road, that type of surprise could always be anticipated. The German command did not allow itself to be overwhelmed. On the way to the small village of Pobolowo, the enemy division was already encountering the lead elements of the approaching motorized infantry division. A difficult night fight ensued. The Bolsheviks employed tanks and a lot of artillery. We let them approach. The German fighting vehicles then thrust into the enemy tanks and artillery.

The battalions approached along different routes. Even for tanks, it was difficult terrain. The routes led through deep sand and morass. It was marshy terrain next to the main road everywhere. The command vehicle of the commander got stuck. The white-haired *Oberstleutnant* accompanied the attack in a *Kübelwagen*. He was the "mover and shaker" among the "black" men[1] of his regiment. They soon encountered the first Soviet tanks, fast vehicles. The lead German company was able to deploy somewhat. The enemy was surprised. Before he was able to fire, a high-explosive round had hit his turret. The vehicle was set ablaze. A second Soviet tank in the village experienced the same fate. We thrust through along the road to Shlobin.

---

1. Translator's Note: German tankers were often referred to as "black" men because of their black uniforms.

In the middle of the road was a firing battery. But it did not hit anything. The German tank rounds shredded the guns, the crews, and the limbers. A confused mass rolled around on the ground. The next battery was in the process of limbering up, when the rounds of the leading fighting vehicles got them. Thirty men were able to save themselves by disappearing behind an embankment off the road. They fired from their cover with rifles. The commander moved towards them in his *Kübelwagen.* Together with his liaison officer and driver, he took the rascals prisoner.

The road from Shlobin, upon which the Soviet division had wanted to break into the rear of the armored division, became the road of its destruction. Infantry attempted to flee into the patches of vegetation and woods to the right and left. But the tank rounds got them quicker that they could run. Bolshevik antitank guns wanted to turn the tables of the calamity. A couple of rounds ricocheted off the armor. A few dents and blemishes were the result. Otherwise nothing. The German steel held. The antitank guns were blown to bits. The infantry of the motorized division greeted the fighting vehicles that had come to their aid with enthusiasm and happiness.

"You can't believe," one of the tank commanders told us later, "how happy we are when we conduct our attack and our infantry are grinning from ear to ear."

A heavy tank company was brought forward to outside of Shlobin. A young *Leutnant* was the acting commander in place of the wounded company commander. The tank commanders stood in their cupolas with a practiced, skilled eye. They were quicker to fire than the Bolsheviks. More Soviet tanks burned. Shlobin and its railway station were reached. The acting company commander saw an armored train in front of him. To the front and rear were rail cars loaded with stones to protect the train against mines. In the middle was the locomotive, along with the armored rail cars. The tanks spread out to attack. Round after round left the main guns. They blew the locomotive to bits and immobilized the train.

The antitank guns of an infantry regiment had also pulled forward with the fighting vehicles and were employed. They took the turrets on the train under fire with great accuracy. Their rounds penetrated. Flames licked out of the destroyed turrets. The tanks advanced as far as the large bridge over the Dnjepr. At the same moment, it went up in the air. The tangle of rails smashed into the Dnjepr with a crash.

It had turned evening. The victorious fighting vehicles of our tank regiment rolled back along sandy trails to their bivouac areas. Without eating or drinking, the tankers had rolled into battle early in the morning. They now displayed a healthy appetite. The black men sat happily together and discussed the details of their great victory. The division commander had already congratulated the *Oberstleutnant.* The after-action reports were collated and the balance sheet reviewed. One battalion by itself had destroyed an armored train, twenty-three tanks, one armored car, four batteries, and seven antitank guns. The report from the other battalion was not yet available. It was still moving on the other side of the main road. But it could be seen from its initial reports that its success had been just as great.

"It'll be thirteen tanks, six batteries, and fifteen antitank guns," the *Oberstleutnant* said with a beaming face. "But let's get some sleep."

In the distance, the rattling of the last tanks died out. Three young armor *Leutnants* sat at a small table with a bottle of wine. It was the last bottle they had put away for just such an occasion.

The flames tongued their way high into the nighttime sky out of the ruins of Rogatschew.

The flaming remains of Rogatschew shone bright and red on the horizon, like a signal flame. Behind them, the Dnjepr was flowing. It had to be forced. It would be.

THE DIVISIONAL HISTORY
The divisional history[2] records the events of this chapter as follows:

At that point, the Russians seized the initiative. Unnoticed, they headed out during the dark and raw night of 5–6 July from Schlobin to a point halfway to the main road. The Soviet 117th Infantry Division had the mission to cut off the *3. Panzer-Division* from its logistics lines of communication at the Dubysna Bridge, over which some 250 vehicles rolled daily. The thrust landed right in the middle of the formations of the *10. Infanterie-Division (mot.),*[3] which were staging for their own attack

---

2. Translator's Note: Traditionsverband, *Geschichte,* 126–28. The reader will note a substantial variance in this account, which also describes the high losses suffered by the 1st Battalion.

3. Translator's Note: The division had just completed its transition to a motorized formation prior to the start of "Barbarossa." As was typical with the early-war motorized infantry divisions, it did not have an organic tank formation. At the time

the next morning. The Soviets were able to penetrate into Pobolowo by surprise and wipe out the elements of the division that were there.

At 0545 hours, the division alerted the *II./Panzer-Regiment 6* for immediate employment in support of the neighboring division. Since the downpours of 5 July had made the unimproved roads almost impassable, the battalion had to first move back five kilometers to get to Pobolowo on secondary roads. All of the wheeled vehicles got stuck in the mud. The regimental headquarters likewise bogged down. *Oberstleutnant* von Lewinski had his command vehicle towed by a fighting vehicle, so as to be able to at least follow the attack, even if he had no way to lead the entire regiment by that means. A simultaneous advance by complete tank battalions in that terrain was barely conceivable. The terrain between the Dnjepr and the Dubysna formed an acute triangle leading to Schlobin. A creek divided this area one more time into two parts. Embankments further restricted the terrain, which offered no extended visibility due to the high corn in the fields.

Without checking with the *3. Panzer-Division*, the command of the *10. Infanterie-Division (mot.)* immediately employed the *I./Panzer-Regiment 6* before the 2nd Battalion had arrived. *Major* Schmidt-Ott advanced with his companies and immediately encountered strong enemy forces. The 1st Company supported the advance of the *II./Infanterie-Regiment (mot.)* on the extreme right wing. The *2./Panzer-Regiment 6* (*Oberleutnant* Buchterkirch) encountered enemy artillery and antitank-gun positions on the high ground southeast of Luki. *Feldwebel* Reinicke, who had lost an arm during the campaign in the West, attacked the batteries, despite their superiority.[4] All by himself, he was able to shoot an entire battery and two additional guns to pieces. The *Panzer III* of *Feldwebel* Machens (Driver: *Gefreiter* Kullrich) was hit in the drive sprocket and immobilized. The crew had to hold out in the tank during the day and was unable to bail out until it turned dark. The tank was recovered during the night.

The *4./Panzer-Regiment 6* (*Oberleutnant* von Brodowski) moved at high speed along a road that was not on the map directly towards Schlobin. All of the company broke through a blocking position with antitank guns,

---

of the actions described here, the division had two motorized rifle regiments (20th and 41st), a motorcycle battalion (40th), a motorized reconnaissance battalion (10th), a motorized artillery regiment (10th), an antitank battalion (10th), a motorized engineer battalion (10th), and the normal divisional troops.

4. Translator's Note: He is the subject of a later chapter.

since it was impossible to leave the road. As a result, one tank followed the other towards Schlobin and the increasingly heavy enemy defensive fires. The Russian guns could barely be identified. In addition, they had camouflaged fighting vehicles in the high corn so well that they were not noticed until their fire broke into the company at pointblank range. The first German tank bogged down and the second one ran over a mine. The next three were shot to pieces by Russian fighting vehicles. The infantry had lagged behind and was prevented from closing with the tanks due to the long-range artillery fire of the Russians. The Soviets concentrated their fires on the fighting vehicles of the 4th Company. When it had moved out that morning, it had thirteen tanks. One after the other was going up in smoke and flame. *Leutnant* von Wedel was killed; a short while later, *Leutnant* Busse as well. *Oberleutnant* von Brodowski died a few days later from the burns he received. Along with him, twenty-two noncommissioned officers and enlisted personnel were killed. Some of the thirty-six remaining were badly wounded. Only three tanks returned from the death march of the 4th Company.

Major Schmidt-Ott ordered his 1st Company forward, which also suffered several losses. The 1st Company provided covering fire so that the remnants of the 4th Company could disengage from the enemy. Individual tanks of the 2nd Company were also there and took their wounded comrades on board, despite the enemy fire. Once again, it was *Feldwebel* Reinicke who distinguished himself. He was the last to leave the battlefield. For his aggressive actions and his already demonstrated performance, the *Feldwebel* received the Knight's Cross.[5]

By noon on that "black" day, the *I./Panzer-Regiment 6* had lost twenty-two fighting vehicles, half of its inventory. The loss could not be balanced by the destruction of nineteen Russian fighting vehicles, twenty-one guns, two antiaircraft guns, and thirteen antitank guns. For the self-sacrificing actions of his battalion, *Major* Schmidt-Ott would later receive mention in the Army Honor Roll.

The *II./Panzer-Regiment 6* heard the cries for help from the 1st Battalion on the radio. *Oberstleutnant* Munzel decided to attack east of the embankment, since he could not provide direct support. The 5th

---

5. Translator's Note: Gerhard Reinicke was submitted for the award on 3 July and received it on 9 July. By the end of the war, he was a *Leutnant*. He passed away in Viersen on 4 July 1997.

Company (*Oberleutnant* Jarosch von Schweder) took the lead, followed closely by the 7th and 8th Companies. Between Tertesch and the railway line, the lead company was able to knock out four enemy batteries, one tank and three antitank guns. The 5th and 7th Companies then covered the advance of the 8th Company (*Leutnant Dr.* Köhler) by leapfrogging. The 8th Company entered the city from the flank and advanced by surprise all the way to the bridge over the Dnjepr. Nonetheless, the enemy was able to blow it up in the nick of time. That meant that a lot of Russians were also still in the city. With his six *Panzer IV's, Leutnant* Dr. Köhler was able to destroy a total of twenty-two Russian tanks, two antitank guns, and one armored train. That meant that the danger of an advance by strong forces from Schlobin was thwarted for the time being.

At 0300 hours during the night, *Panzer-Regiment 6* sent its recovery platoon out onto the battlefield, covered by the regimental light platoon, to recover its shot-up fighting vehicles. The work lasted through the entire next day. The men of the maintenance facility and the maintenance sections did not get any rest. *Leutnant* Jacobs, who covered the recovery operations with his light platoon, shot up an additional four enemy antitank guns.

THE HISTORY OF *PANZER-REGIMENT 6*
The regimental history[6] of *Panzer-Regiment 6* records the events of this chapter as follows:

On 6 July, the entire regiment was alerted at 0515 hours. It was directed to assist the *10. Infanterie-Division (mot.),* which was involved in heavy fighting. That division had run into heavy enemy forces during its advance on Slobin at night. Its lead battalion had suffered extremely heavy casualties. Many soldiers had been massacred in the most despicable way. Apparently, the enemy had the intention of cutting off our division, whereupon he ran into the other division.

The 1st Battalion was sent directly towards Slobin by the division. The 2nd Company (*Oberleutnant* Buchterkirch) took the lead and was able to eliminate artillery and antitank guns. But when it approached the city of Slobin, however, it encountered numerous well-camouflaged tanks and antitank guns among the houses and gardens. Hemmed in by the nature of the terrain, it was not able to bring its full firepower to bear. Fighting to

6. Translator's Note: Munzel, *Gekämpft, gesiegt, verloren,* 74–78.

its front, it was suddenly also engaged from the rear by guns and antitank guns that had been overrun but whose crews, which had hidden in the woods, had returned to their weapons. The 4th Company, off to the right, then advanced. But the enemy resistance was so strong that it also suffered extremely heavy casualties in a short period. *Leutnant* von Wedel and *Leutnant* Busse were killed, along with twenty-six noncommissioned officers and men. The commander of the 4th Company, *Oberleutnant* von Brodowski, was so badly wounded that he soon died. An additional thirty-six noncommissioned officers and men were more or less badly wounded. Twenty-two tanks of the battalion were put out of commission. The commander, *Oberstleutnant* Schmidt-Ott, who was personally participating in the attack, brought his 1st Company forward. It also lost several tanks. But under its covering fires, the remnants of the forward companies could pull back, in the process of which *Feldwebel* Reinicke especially distinguished himself by recovering a number of crewmembers who had bailed out. Although the battalion was able to destroy nineteen tanks, eleven heavy and ten light guns, two antiaircraft guns, and thirteen antitank guns, the price for it was too high.

A participant in the fighting, the former *Funkmeister* Heinz Krüger,[7] has provided his account:

> The 4th Company was the lead element of the 1st Battalion. It moved well ahead of the friendly infantry. When we emerged from under a railway crossing with the company commander's tank, there were two tanks moving ahead of us, those of *Feldwebel* Molde and *Feldwebel* Köller. Both of them immediately attempted to get off of the road and into the adjacent fields, but they ran over mines in the process. Molde was also captured, but he returned a few days later. There was no trace of the other crewmembers. We were thus forced to continue to attack along the road and received terrible fire from artillery pieces and skillfully camouflaged T-34's in the high corn. It was our first encounter with this type of tank. A round penetrated our tank from the front at the driver's station. The vehicle immediately started to burn. Only *Oberleutnant von Brodowski* and I at the radio station

---

7. Translator's Note: A *Funkmeister* was the equivalent of a *Feldwebel* within the signal corps.

emerged alive, before the tank exploded and the turret went next to the chassis. I had 2nd and 3rd degree burns on my face and arms; I also received artillery shrapnel in the left lower thigh and in the arms while lying in the open between my comrades. After several attempts, *Unteroffizier* Borowczek succeeded in dragging me past the burning tank to his *Panzer II*. He took me back to the railway crossing, thus saving my life. The driver of the staff car, who was supposed to take me to the main clearing station, ran over a friendly mine in the next locality. It had been placed in the open by the infantry, in case the Russians broke through. I was flung out of the vehicle; the driver was instantly killed. An infantry officer loaded me into his vehicle and took me to the clearing station.

☩

A second account, this one by *Gefreiter* Haas from the 2nd Company, states the following concerning the fighting and heavy losses of the 1st Battalion:

The initial fighting in the east was behind us. In and around our tanks for the last fifteen days, we had grown older. Up to then, the advance through Brest-Litowsk, Kobryn, Buchowiza, the Sczara, Filipowicze, Slusk, Brobruisk, the Beresina, and as far as Rogatschew had only cost us three dead and six wounded and the total loss of three tanks.

It was Sunday, 6 July, 0430 hours. We were ready to roll out. After a short, restless night in our quartering village of Kaschari, we were once again in firing range of the enemy artillery. A large expanse of marshland extended in front of us. There was something in the air. The mission we had been given for the day stated we were to turn back a Russian attack across the Dnjepr against the *10. Infanterie-Division*. We raced down the road twenty-five kilometers in that direction. We were sitting outside on our fighting vehicles. Then we received a radio message from our company commander, "Indigo": "Slobin in front of us. The leader of 'Vulkan' [the 1st Battalion] directs us farther forward. Turn back the enemy infantry attack."

We increased our speed. As far as we could see, there was Russian infantry in our sights. The Russians were advancing in several waves against our riflemen.

We then went through a railway viaduct towards our attack objective.

We received a new order from "Indigo" as we were in the process of engaging enemy artillery: "Stop engagement. Take up old direction of march. Head towards Slobin."

We then had to come to the aid our beloved commander, *Major* Schmidt-Ott. He had encountered heavy enemy resistance on the edge of Slobin with the 4th Company. Since he only had a dummy main gun and a machine gun in his command vehicle, his situation had become extremely critical.

The platoon leader vehicle of the 2nd Platoon (*Feldwebel* Machens) received a direct hit from artillery in front of the viaduct, which tore off the drive sprocket. Despite that, he continued to engage additional nests of artillery and infantry with his vehicle, without regard for the numerous impacts around it.

Feldwebel Weide assumed command of the 2nd Platoon. We engaged enemy pockets of resistance while moving past them. Despite that, Russians infiltrated to our rear from all sides, so that we were soon receiving fire from the front and rear. We had landed in an inferno, in which only cold-bloodedness was a guarantee for survival.

But it was imperative to free our commander from his threatening situation. It took a lot of effort to work our way up to him. Vehicle 201, *Feldwebel* Weide, received antitank-gun and artillery hits in the process. His driver, *Gefreiter* Oldendorf, died. The remaining crew bailed out. The vehicle continued to move slowly forward. Vehicle 214, *Unteroffizier* Söllner, identified enemy tanks in some outbuildings in front of us. They were skillfully camouflaged and hard to make out. The company headquarters, with vehicles 200 and 201, immediately took the tanks under fire. 214 received orders to move forward under covering fire from 201 and enable the battalion commander to pull back

All of a sudden, two tankers raced across the terrain, which was full of impacting rounds, towards the wooden outbuildings. It was the two officer candidates, *Gefreiter* von Bieler and *Gefreiter* Redderberg. They succeeded in putting two of the tanks, which had not been prepared for that type of move, out of commission with hand grenades. While hurrying back, *Gefreiter* Rüdiger von Bieler was killed by an antitank-gun round.

The call from our company commander echoed through the radio over and over again: "Indigo leader to all stations . . . where is Busse? Where is Machens? Over . . . over!"

There was nothing to be seen or heard of the three platoon leaders in the heavy fire. That didn't give you a good feeling.

The enemy had set up a trap for us by means of deep tank ditches on both sides of the improved road. The Russian guns had registered along the road. The effort to get across the ditch did not succeed. The tank of *Leutnant* von Kriegsheim was already stuck in it. We therefore had to cross the intersection, which was under heavy fire. There was no other way. We did it individually without incident and then deployed out again.

Vehicle 212 was knocked out on a slight rise. The company commander's vehicle was 100 meters farther forward, likewise knocked out. Vehicles 201 and 214 pulled up next to it and opened fire on four antitank guns and an artillery piece 300 meters distant. The tank commander of 214 radioed to the adjutant, *Leutnant* Adameck: "Pull back immediately! I'll cover!"

While pulling back, *Leutnant* Adameck identified another antitank gun, which had fired at the battalion commander's vehicle. *Gefreiter* Sawallisch, the gunner on 214, was able to put that one out of commission. 214 then pulled back and received a few antitank-gun hits in the process, but they did not cause any special damage. Vehicle 201 was able to knock that antitank gun out in the nick of time.

Despite the heavy enemy fire, *Gefreiter* Haas and *Gefreiter* Strawinski jumped out of their tank in order to recover the badly wounded, and left behind, *Feldwebel* Weide. By dint of great effort, they placed him on the rear deck of their tank. After they had succeeded in doing that, they jumped down again to save other tankers stranded out front. No comrade was to fall into the hands of the enemy alive.

While the combat elements of the 2nd Company freed the battalion commander, our *Hauptfeldwebel*,[8] *Unteroffizier* Rohloff, and *Unteroffizier* Götz raced to the railway embankment in the commander's *Kübelwagen* under heavy enemy fire to come to the assistance of the tank on fire at the viaduct. They were greeted by a horrific scene. The comrades, some of them still on board, some of them in the road ditch, were badly wounded. They were given field dressings as quickly as possible. But without help from tanks, no one else could be recovered. The three men in the *Kübelwagen* raced back to get help from the vehicles of the 1st Company. The men of that company immediately joined the fray. They attempted another advance, but they were turned back. *Funkmeister* Schmitt was killed in the attempt; *Gefreiter* Nürnberg was badly wounded and later died of his wounds.

A radio message from the battalion—'*Vulkan*'—ordered the immediate disengagement from the enemy, moving back 800 meters along the road. Our Company Commander also issued orders to recover all the wounded and take them along.

Vehicle 201 with *Feldwebel* Reinicke moved back to the place where *Gefreiter* von Bieler had fallen. *Gefreiter* Haas removed his identity disk[9] and looked for other wounded. *Gefreiter* Wellner could be evacuated from the driver's station of 214, badly wounded. Also wounded, *Gefreiter* Übelacker drove his own tank—201—to the rear. The vehicles took wounded from both the 1st and 4th Companies with them. The crew of 211, *Feldwebel* Machens, bailed out of its combat-ineffective vehicle. It took the most important things with it: Weapons, portions of the main gun breechblock, radio transmitter, communications instructions, per-

---

8. Translator's Note: *Hauptfeldwebel* was a function and not a rank. The *Hauptfeldwebel* is equivalent to the U.S. Army's first sergeant.

9. Translator's Note: Like the U.S. Army, the German Army also used identity disks—*Erkennungsmarken*—for identifying the fallen. The German version contained the blood group, a roll number (usually from the unit to which the soldier was first assigned when entering the army), and the unit itself. The information was embossed on the metal oval tag twice, with one piece to remain with the soldier and the other to be taken for accountability purposes in case of death on the battlefield.

sonal items. Vehicles 211, 235, 241 and 101 remained behind on the battlefield on that difficult day of fighting. The wounded were collected at the clearing stating at Fedabowka-Belischka. The battalion set up all-round security.

As was later determined, the battalion suffered the following losses: thirty-one dead and three missing.

The company commander of the 4th Company died eight days later as a result of his bad burns.

From the ranks of the 2nd Company, the following men died at Slobin: *Leutnant* von Wedel, *Leutnant* Busse, *Gefreiter* von Bieler, *Gefreiter* Ollendorf, *Gefreiter* Klein, *Gefreiter* Schwaiger, *Obergefreiter* Zimmermann, *Panzerschütze* Schenk, and *Gefreiter* Bartels.

Leutnant von Wedel fell out of comradeship to *Leutnant* Busse. Busse's legs had been shot off in the tank. *Leutnant* von Wedel climbed down from his tank to help apply field dressings. During the effort to recover him, von Wedel, who had positioned himself over the badly wounded man to protect him, was surrounded by enemy infantry. Busse's request of von Wedel—that he should get himself to safety, since he was bleeding to death—was not honored by that noble man. Von Wedel did not want his comrade to fall into enemy hands. A sniper mortally wounded him. As a result, both of the young officers of the company lost their lives.

Under the cover of night, a patrol from our company went out onto the battlefield one more time to recover the dead. *Leutnant* Jakobs found both of the officers in front of the bridge. *Leutnant* von Wedel still had his submachine gun at the ready. A bullet had struck the heart of the best of officers.

Our *Gefreiter* Herbert Müller dedicated himself to a Russian peasant woman, who had been wounded in the upper thigh, treating her with a great deal of care.

While that fight was going on, the 2nd Battalion was still on its approach march. Although it heard the radio traffic of the 1st Battalion, it was unable to offer rapid assistance due to the streaming rain and an impassable railway embankment. Should it turn around to try to use another route behind the 1st Battalion or should it attempt to make a parallel advance and envelop the enemy? The battalion commander decided on the last measure, since that would get his battalion to the objective faster. The 5th Company took the lead. In the process, it encountered more enemy and eliminated four batteries, one tank and three antitank guns.

The 8th Company then moved forward and, under the aggressive leadership of *Leutnant der Reserve* Dr. Köhler, advanced into the city, knocking out twenty-two enemy tanks with his six *Panzer IV's*. He also brought a train to a standstill that was attempting to flee to safety to the east across the Dnjepr. Unfortunately, the bridge went up in the air right in front of the first friendly tank. But the small city was firmly in our hands, and the danger of a strong Russian attack against the *10. Infanterie-Division (mot.)* and the right flank of our division eliminated. The *10. Infanterie-Division (mot.)* could occupy the west bank of the Dnjepr at that point, and the tanks that were scattered outside of Slobin could be recovered. In the process, *Leutnant* Jakobs and his light platoon were able to take out four antitank guns that had been crewed again. Among the friction of war of that day was the fact that the regimental headquarters, which was to coordinate the fight in a unified manner, had gotten bogged down along a marshy route and did not reach the battlefield until everything was over. All elements of the regiment then returned to their quartering areas. *Oberstleutnant* Schmidt-Ott, whose dummy main gun had been completely deformed, was mentioned in the "Honor Roll of the Army" for his self-sacrificing actions. *Generalleutnant* Model viewed the war materiel that had been destroyed by the battalion a day later. It was the most severe casualties suffered by the 1st Battalion up to that point.

Our "Tank Road" leads through a village of the Soviet paradise. The vehicles have had a conspicuous "G" added to them, indicating they are part of *Panzergruppe Guderian*.

On to the Beresina through burning woods.

On the Dnjepr. Combat engineers attempt to salvage whatever they can for restoring the original span.

A day of rain suffices to turn the roads into a bed of clay. Since few of the roads were what the military considered "improved"—that is, have asphalt surfaces—this is what most of the forces in the field encountered whenever there was anything more than a light rain. The roads of the rural Soviet Union at the time were never intended for such traffic.

Even along the Dnjepr, there was heavy fighting in the built-up areas.

And in the industrial facilities.

The dismounted lead elements feel their way through a contested village.

The railway bridge over the Dnjepr was destroyed by the Soviets. Engineers erect a new bridge next to it, over which the division rolls.

A section of Bolsheviks who had been directed to defend the blown-up footbridge surrenders.

Forward across the finished bridge over the Dnjepr.

The enemy is ejected on the far side of the Dnjepr.

The Bolsheviks burned down a bridge along the road . . .

. . . but our engineers conjured up a new one in short order.

Infantry and armor advance across an open area. The tank is a *Panzer 35(t)*, which was a Czech vehicle manufactured at the Skoda works and impressed into service into the *Panzerwaffe* due to the perennial shortfall of armored vehicles and the rapid expansion of the *Panzerwaffe* in 1940. The *Panzer 35(t)* had a 3.7-centimeter main gun and relatively thin and brittle armor. It was quickly phased out of service early in the war.

A command and artillery observation post.

CHAPTER 9

Across the Dnjepr through the Stalin Line

RUSSIA'S SECOND-LARGEST RIVER BEHIND US

A sticky evening followed a glowing hot day.[1] In the sun, the temperature had registered 42 degrees (107 Fahrenheit). With a magnificent display of color such as you wouldn't believe if a painter had painted it, the moon replaced the sun. Initially, it was paper lantern turning from red to yellow barely above the crowns of the dark firs and the high spruces. Then it was a light arc lamp in the moving clouds of the heavens. But its light did not help much that night. Columns moved along sandy secondary roads that were saturated with deep craters. They churned up powdery dust mixed with the milky vapors that were climbing from the wet, marshy meadows. The drivers could not afford to lose sight of the man ahead of them. Only the small illuminated bars of the night driving lights provided any direction.

The deep rumbling of powerful engines, the rattling of tracks, the hard pounding of large wheels—sounds we had grown accustomed to over the days—pulsated across the landscape in front of the Dnjepr flood plain. Heavy artillery moved into position, frequently in two columns next to one another. Occasionally, there was one of the usual deadlocks that come about during those types of difficult marches. Then, all of a sudden, there was an uncanny quiet that descended over the column. One time, the sounds of ever-approaching engine noises echoed down from the heavens. Enemy pilots looking for nighttime targets. The word passed quickly: "Night lights out!" The small lights were extinguished. The sound of the aircraft grew distant. The column had not been discovered. Like a parade

---

1. Translator's Note: This particular chapter does not directly cover the actions of the *3. Panzer-Division*. Instead, it concerns the operations of the *4. Panzer-Division* in forcing the Dnjepr at Stary Bychow (Starbychow in the text). Hence, there are no regimental or divisional excerpts at the end of this section.

of eerie shadows and unreal silhouettes—that was the way batteries moved off of the route in the nighttime darkness and into pre-determined areas for the firing positions.

The messenger who was to lead us to the observation post of the heavy howitzer battery waited for us at the railway embankment, just outside of the small town of Starbychow. It was past midnight, and the first light of the next morning started to arrive. We went along a field trail through high rye. A narrow communications trench led in a zigzag fashion to the dug-out observation post of the battery commander in the middle of the grain. Another day of decision had arrived on that morning, 10 July. When the heavy howitzers behind us in their firing positions opened their roaring mouths in the chorus of guns and cannon, that would signal the assault across the Dnjepr at a place where the Bolsheviks least expected a German attack. There were still a few hours until then. But no one was thinking of sleep. We talked quietly about the previous engagements and about the coming large-scale attack. It would succeed—all of us were convinced of that. A few hundred meters in front of us, in the bottom of the valley, the Dnjepr flowed.

This was the big picture:

Beyond Brobruisk on the Beresina, the broad avenue of advance—on which the divisions of our armored corps in the first days of July had stormed towards, the Dnjepr—forked. On the upper arm of the large fork that led to the northeast was the city of Mogilew. It was an important industrial center with numerous military facilities. It was still in the hands of the Soviets. The lower tine of the fork, running directly west to east, was Rogatschew, which had already been taken in hard fighting. By then, it had been reduced to a burned-down pile of rubble. Four traffic routes connected those two cities, which were separated by about ninety kilometers from north to south: the broad band of the Dnjepr; a railway line; and two roads, one on this side of the river and one on the far side.

The armored corps had thrust into that operationally important triangle—Brobruisk, Mogilew, and Rogatschew—which was formed by the main roads and the Dnjepr, like a spread-out thumb and index finger. It was there that its divisions had to force a crossing over the second-largest river of Russia. After the Bug and the Beresina, an extraordinarily difficult mission. The German command had no doubts at all about that. River crossings by armored divisions are among their most difficult missions. In addition, at the Dnjepr, the German forces had run into the "Stalin Line," which ran from the Black Sea to the Gulf of Finland. The river itself formed a decisive part of the defensive network.

The attack was prepared with the thoroughness that is unique to us Germans. The strength and intentions of the enemy were extensively examined. From the many mosaic stones that reconnaissance provided, a picture of the enemy situation started to be formed. It was soon clear to the command that the areas around Mogilew and Rogatschew had been expanded into strong bulwarks of the Dnjepr Line. German aerial reconnaissance had noted wide-scale troop movements. Until recently, the pilots had observed reinforcements rolling along the east bank towards Mogilew. The statements of many prisoners and deserters completed the picture. The Bolsheviks had brought up fresh divisions, including several artillery regiments. There were approximately two corps around Mogilew and one around Rogatschew—forces from central Russia, the broad Volga area, and the Ukraine. They had been standing by for the planned attack on Germany. Together with elements of the divisions that had streamed back, been battered, or been wiped out, they were to prevent the crossing over the Dnjepr in strong field fortifications with all the means at their disposal.

The gigantic river basin of the Dnjepr, with its innumerable large and small tributaries, creeks, and dead branches, was marshy and miry. Its flood plains—open for kilometers at a stretch, overgrown and full of twists and turns—presented the attacker with a difficult obstacle. For motorized formations, it appeared to be uncrossable.

The Bolsheviks attempted to transition to counterattacks from the bridgeheads. But they were unable to divert the German leadership from its goal. Without regard for the Soviet actions, it looked for the weakest point in the "Stalin Line." The headquarters staffs pored over maps and reconnaissance material until late into the night. The weak spot was found. Following that, the German command worked quickly and decisively. The armored spearhead spread out. In remarkably short time, the approach march was completed along the few roads. Almost in the middle between Rogatschew and Mogilew was the small city of Starbychow, on this side of the river. It had also gone up in flames due to enemy artillery fire. It was only at the edges that a few buildings were still standing. Five German fighting vehicles had attempted to take the wooden bridge over the Dnjepr there in a bold *coup de main* in the first week of July. They had barely crossed over to the vegetation on the far side when the bridge behind them went up in the air. The Bolsheviks had prepared it for demolition. The fighting vehicles were cut off. In an adventurous escape, most of the tankers succeeded in making it back across the Dnjepr.[2] The front was relatively quiet there. The Soviets felt secure in the cover of the marshy flood plain. At intervals, the Bolshevik artillery fired into the city and the surrounding villages. German outposts had carefully worked their way up to the river.

The German command placed the main effort of its offensive in the sector around Starbychow. Our armored division pushed its way along secondary roads from the main route, through villages and woods, on the evening and night of 8–9 July to its staging areas. The opportunities for cover and concealment in that wooded terrain also worked to the advantage of the attacker. While other divisions screened in the direction of Mogilew and Rogatschew, it was directed for the rifle brigade to cross the Dnjepr early on 10 July in inflatable craft and, upstream on the Dnjepr at Starbychow, establish a strong bridgehead. The artillery plan was worked out to the last detail. The bridging site, the order of crossing and the individual timelines. That's how certain the German command was of its success.

The inflatable craft were blown up. The guns elevated skyward; the batteries waited for their firing missions. Whoever looked across the sun-drenched river valley of the Dnjepr that morning could not possibly imagine how a monstrous burst of fire would shatter the stillness in a few minutes. Nothing could be seen. Despite that, hundreds of pairs of eye, just like ours, were searching the woods on the far side. Riflemen and motorcycle infantry, antitank crewmen, and combat engineers were all lying at the wait a few hundred meters from the banks. The arms of scissor scopes, wrapped in stalks of grain, were carefully raised above the waving stems of the rye. The section of meadowland on the far side appeared to be a good four kilometers wide, as it stretched out between the river and the woods. Scattered in there were numerous groups of vegetation with

---

2. Translator's Note: The author has his rivers mixed up, perhaps intentionally in the interest of operational security. He is recounting the story of *Oberleutnant* von Cossel and his platoon from *Panzer-Regiment 35 (4. Panzer-Division)* crossing the Drut. It was, in fact, the same division that reached the Dnjepr at Stary Bychow and forced a crossing there with its motorcycle battalion.

Bolshevik foxholes and machine-gun nests. The assaulting riflemen had
to move through that terrain. The battery commander checked his map
one more time. The identified targets, which his heavy howitzers would
hammer, had been marked. Over the last few days, the range-finding
batteries had identified the enemy artillery positions by means of light and
sound measuring. He then issued the order to fire.

Powerful thunderclaps . . . twitching flashes of lightning . . . balls of fire
shooting high everywhere . . . they transformed the slumbering valley into
a raging witch's cauldron. The new attack rolled, almost as if on schedule.
Right to the minute, the *Stukas* plunged from the heavens and the fighters
sang their high-pitched engine song. But no enemy pilot allowed himself
to be seen. The destructive hail of our artillery fire hammered into the
groups of vegetation and the woods, holding down the enemy with its
intensity. Powerful and grandiose were the uninterrupted rising and
falling howling and gurgling sounds of the rounds that combed through
all of the woods on the other side. Then there was the hissing and rushing
sound of the new weapon. Steep trails of smoke arched skywards. Thick
banks of artificial smoke robbed the enemy of his visibility. The German
artillery had placed a blazing curtain of fire in front of the woods on the
far side.

Two strong *Kampfgruppen* moved out to conduct the assault. The
command post for one of them was in the brickworks with the high
chimney next to our observation post. With the natural self-sacrificing
nature of the German soldier, the riflemen and engineers moved out
towards the river with the onset of the artillery fire. It was difficult to run
with the cumbersome watercraft. The soldiers gasped and steamed. It was
five in the morning, but the Russian summer was hot.

The leadership had taken thorough precautionary measures.
Numerous pneumatic craft were paddled across the slow-flowing river. It
almost looked like some sort of noble competition. The companies had to
cross all at once so that appreciable combat formations could immediately
advance towards the woods on the far bank. The shore was flat and sandy.
The first battalion crossed in short order. The regimental commander
immediately followed. The rounds crashed into the trees with unabated
fury. Whatever Bolshevik had not been hit was pressing himself deep into
his foxhole. The riflemen were assaulting right behind the creeping fire
through the meadows and the marshes and into the woods. The enemy

was overrun by the first assault wave. The staccato beat of a few individual machine guns echoed our way. The first prisoners were brought back. Many of them were wounded—proof of how well the artillery fires had been placed.

The first part of the attack had succeeded. The Dnjepr had been forced. The second assault wave crossed the river. Suddenly, fire from enemy machine-gun nests. A few nests fired from the flanks. They had previously remained silent. They were quickly finished off. The Soviet artillery started firing. Individual rounds landed next to the approach routes and on the forward slopes of the artillery observation posts. The brickworks started to burn, but the command post had long since moved to the far bank. The assault craft were shoved into the water. The sweat was pouring out of the engineers. Four men each carried the heavy craft. Ferries were constructed. The work went swiftly from the practiced hands of the soldiers. At this point, the river was eighty meters wide; motor ferries were soon chugging across. A corduroy road was built across the soft meadowlands. The heavy infantry weapons were crossed, antitank guns and infantry guns. Prime movers followed. Only occasionally did a light artillery round fall on this side of the Dnjepr. The crossing traffic remained uninterrupted. The sound of the fighting was soon coming from the woods. The engineers wiped the sweat from their glistening faces. After the hard work, they were happy to be relieved. Morale was high along the Dnjepr. More and more prisoners came streaming out of the woods.

"Twelve more on 8800!" the battery commander ordered his *Leutnant* in the battery position. The wall of fire kept advancing. During the morning hours, the riflemen worked their way towards the main road that connected Mogilew and Rogatschew on the east bank of the Dnjepr. The route the Bolsheviks had previously used for reinforcements had been cut. The riflemen began advancing down that route. The battery changed positions forward. The forward observer went with a radio section to the front lines. The main road south and east of Starbychow was blocked by German artillery fire.

Just before one in the afternoon, the Bolsheviks attempted a thrust into the flanks against the ferry point. We suddenly saw two strong columns break out of the woods to the right. But the forward observer for a howitzer battery issued a fire mission as quick as lightning. The rounds slammed into the middle of the throng of Bolsheviks. The rounds, intended as ricochets, exploded high in the air. It must have been terrible. The Bolsheviks threw themselves to the ground. A couple ran back. The howitzer battery fired at a rapid rate. In a few moments, a drama had taken place in front of our eyes. Then the fire jumped over to the bridge embankment. The observer had discovered enemy there as well.

In the meantime, the riflemen fought their way down the road. They then swung back to the west onto the road that led to Starbychow along an embankment. The motorcycle infantry approached them through the burned-down city. The bridge was to be erected there. The engineer vehicles approached with their large pontoons. A day later, the mighty army would continue its thrust into the Bolshevik front.

At the division command post, the reports of victory along the Dnjepr filtered in. The second *Kampfgruppe*, which had been employed farther up the river, had also been able to force it in the covering fire provided by the artillery. It had erected a 100-meter footbridge over rubber boats. It had also advanced quickly through the woods to the main road. However, it was receiving heavy artillery fire from the woods on the far side of the road. *Stukas* were requested. A short while later, gigantic clouds of smoke climbed out of the patch of woods. The bombs had carved out a path for the riflemen.

The division translator interrogated captured Soviet officers. They were no longer wearing rank insignia. Despite that, they were easy to spot. Their statements confirmed that the German attack at that location had come completely unexpectedly and utterly by surprise. The Bolsheviks assumed that there were only weak German outposts were at Starbychow. Because of that, they had planned their own flank thrust there. At an orders conference, everything had been discussed in detail. The Bolshevik advance had been planned for 10 July. But it had to be postponed because—the shrugging of the shoulders by the Bolshevik officer said a lot—the requested aviation support was not ready.

The steely band of armor and motorized divisions rolled across the pontoon bridge at Starbychow. The point of the steel wedge, the incomparable German assault soldier, had advanced farther in heavy fighting.

The strength of the Bolshevik air force—we saw it more and more each day—had been shattered. Along the Beresina, one bomb squadron after the other had attempted to destroy the bridgehead in wave after wave.

Along the Dnjepr, there were only a few bombers that attempted to attack. Their bombs fell widely scattered. The fighters shot a few burning "Red Stars" out of the skies. It was Mölders's famous wing, which had swept the skies clean over Brobruisk. Quick as an arrow, the air over the Dnepr was covered in large circles, watching over us. They waited in vain for the enemy, however. Below them, the large German march columns headed for the main route of advance, which the Bolsheviks at Rogatschew had wanted to prevent. That was the meaning of the Dnjepr crossing and the breakthrough through the "Stalin Line" at Starbychow, a memorable day of the campaign.

Guderian and Model.

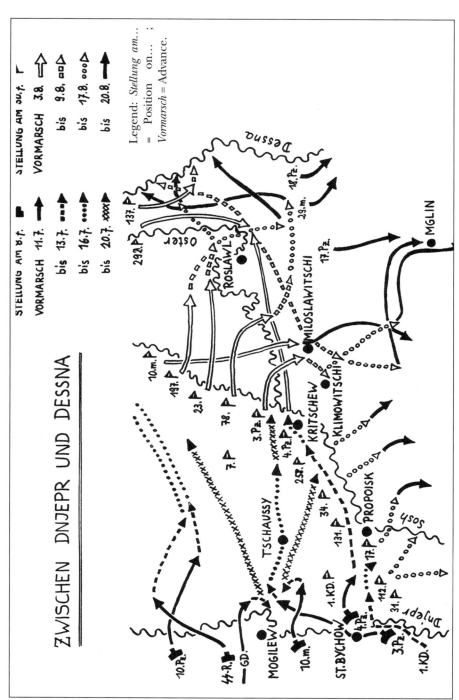

Between the Dnjepr and the Dessna.

CHAPTER 10

One-armed Tank Commander

KNIGHT'S CROSS AND THE JOYS OF FATHERHOOD

When I mounted the company commander's tank before the breakthrough and pursuit of more than 1,000 kilometers along the Schtschara, the company commander pointed out the tank ahead of ours. It was echeloned next to the tank of *Leutnant* Busse, which had just decided the fighting at Shlobin. In the cupola of the tank was a *Feldwebel*, thin and angular, who had an energetic face. One of his arms hung down limply. "That's one of my best," he said. "With Busse and Reinicke[1] up front, nothing much can happen. They are both such old hands at tanking, so quick and decisive in their decisions, so tuned in to the entire 'game of war,' that things would have to go to hell in a hand basket, if we didn't kick the Bolshevik's butt today."

That's how I learned about the nimble man from Berlin, who saw the first light of day in the *Reich* capital on 11 April 1914 and was a businessman, until he went to *Reiter-Regiment 4* in Potsdam in 1934, before it became a tank regiment. In the West, where he drove a smaller tank, he received both the Iron Cross, Second Class, and Iron Cross, First Class, at Ernage. He was also promoted from *Unteroffizier* to *Feldwebel*. Of the six tanks employed there that day, four had been knocked out, including the tank of his former platoon leader and current company commander. Reinicke assumed command of the remaining two tanks, blew apart three French antitank guns, and fought it out with French tanks until his tank was finally also knocked out in the face of numerical superiority. The two comrades with him were killed. Badly wounded, his arm shattered, he bailed out and reached the last operational tank through hammering machine-gun fire, whereupon he was taken to the clearing station, where he was saved, except for the arm, which was lost in the tank engagement of Ernage.

---

1. Translator's Note: This is the same Gerhard Reinicke mentioned in chapter 8.

But his major successes started with the campaign in the East. In a tough attack against enemy gun positions, which were attempting to block the path of our armor division at an important river crossing, he shot to pieces four heavy 10.5-centimeter guns all by himself in a nighttime engagement. Then, riding point, he was the mainstay of the attack for more than 100 kilometers at Sluzk. In the process, six antitank guns, two tanks, and two guns remained behind on the route, all victims of his tank alone. From that point, only a few days separated the start of the heavy fighting at Shlobin, where manly courage had to be employed to the utmost in knocking out extremely heavy concentrations of enemy antitank guns and artillery pieces in turning back the threatened flanking of the division as a consequence of an immediate enemy counterattack across the Dnjepr. Once again, Reinicke was up front; once again, the gods of war smiled upon him. One battery was silenced under the rapid fire of his tank; two tanks were set alight by his main gun; and two more armored vehicles had to give up the fight when high-explosive rounds caused the crews to scatter.

For Reinicke, it goes without saying that tankers dismount to evacuate wounded comrades, even though it demands a lot of you to climb out from behind the protective steel plate in heavy enemy machine-gun fire. What *Feldwebel* Reinicke had done once before—pistol always at the ready on his belt to be able to use it against the enemy with his remaining hand—he did again during the armored engagement outside of Shlobin. When only three fighting vehicles out the original number that had been engaged were still firing towards the end of the heavy fighting, Reinicke picked up a company commander from his battalion, whose vehicle had been knocked out, and another man. He then fired with everything he had, until the last resistance was broken and the enemy retreated across the Dnjepr in wild flight. It was not until then that he left the battlefield as the last tank. He doesn't talk a lot, that *Feldwebel* Reinicke. He is the man known within the regiment, indeed in the entire division, as the one-armed tank commander. He is not a "typical Berliner." He doesn't like to talk about his successes and is thus similar to all tankers, who would rather act than talk. But he did have one worry? "Did my wife have the baby? I've been waiting so long for the news . . ." On the day that the division commander presented him with the Knight's Cross, he also discovered that he had become a father.

Knight's Cross and fatherhood on the same day! Based on the beaming face of the tank commander, you couldn't ask for anything more.

CHAPTER 11

Mogilew

WOUNDED EVACUATED IN HEAVY MACHINE-GUN FIRE

The Soviets attempted again and again to escape envelopment and destruction by means of desperate breakout attempts and attacks against the flanks of our divisions pressing far to the front. On the evening of 11 July, our armor division on the Dnjepr received orders to interdict a threat to the flanks by a large enemy force, beat it back and thus screen the Dnjepr crossing of the armor corps. The reorganization was completed during the night, and the approach march of the division for its attack commenced during the earliest of hours the following morning. Advancing rapidly, the lead elements of the massed enemy forces were overrun. One pocket of resistance after the other was eliminated and two . . . three . . . four villages taken. It appeared that there would not be any obstacles to our attack. But then some heavy "fireworks" suddenly appeared. It was whistling, zinging, and crashing from every nook and cranny at the lead tank companies, which were far ahead of the following rifle companies. It appeared the Soviets had transformed our attack objective into a fortress over the last few days. Automatic weapons, antitank guns, and artillery pieces were positioned everywhere in the bushes and plots of vegetation, in holes in the ground, and in bunkers. They had opened fire with everything they had against our tanks.

The order had already been issued two hours ago alerting the heavy tank company to be prepared for enemy contact. In the acting company commander's tank, the heavy gun had been pre-loaded, and the gunner constantly looked though his gun-sight optics for targets in the enemy-controlled terrain, especially antitank guns.[1] The loader already had his

---

1. Translator's Note: In many postwar accounts, Germans expressed more concern about identifying and eliminating antitank guns than enemy tanks. This was primarily due to the fact that they were almost impossible to identify before they fired, and by then, it was often too late.

next round at the ready, and the radio operator worked ceaselessly at his station monitoring the radio traffic of the battalion and the neighboring companies and also transmitting the commands of the acting company commander to his tanks. The young tank commander stood in the open cupola. He had been leading the company for two weeks, after the company commander had been wounded on the third day of the campaign. He issued constant orders to his platoons and the individual tanks, provided reports to the battalion, and issued directives to his driver through the intercom. The driver of the tank sat down below, a narrow vision port in front of him. His fists were grasping the shifting and braking controls, with which he drove and steered the armored monster. Crouching between the radio operator and the loader was a war correspondent, practically incapable of movement. There was a feverish excitement in the tank, which was suddenly released when the first burst of Bolshevik machine-gun fire sprayed past the tank and then, shortly afterwards, two rounds from an antitank gun whistled past. The rounds were coming from the edge of a locality about 800 meters distant. At the same moment, however—turrets oriented on the houses and vegetation along the edge of the village— the tanks were already firing round after round from their main guns. A quarter of an hour later there was only a burning village in front of them, from which no more antitank guns or machine guns were firing.

The acting company commander was just in the process of issuing orders to continue the advance when orders reached him to assist the neighboring company, which was involved in heavy fighting, on the left. Under the covering fires of one platoon, the company swung in the direction of a railway embankment, behind which our comrades were fighting against enemy artillery, antitank guns and tanks. Our tank company moved up to the railway embankment on a broad front and immediately opened fire on the enemy positions.

In order to get a better field of fire, our tanks changed positions. All of a sudden, there was an ear-deafening detonation . . . muck . . . haze . . . smoke . . . shrapnel. All swept through our tank, which was tossed up under the pressure of the explosion and then landed, immobilized. The *Leutnant,* who was standing at his station, flew through the air in a high arc. The remaining men got out of the tank in a few seconds. Only the driver couldn't do it on his own; he was pulled out by the gunner and the radio operator. He was barely out, when there was another banging and crashing against our tank. Antitank-gun rounds! At the same time, the Soviet showered us with bursts of machine-gun fire.

Our driver was badly wounded in the arms and legs; the gunner had shrapnel in his upper body, and the loader in his left leg. The loader had also received some shrapnel. If only there weren't any damned machine-gun fire! Additional wounds were received. Despite the machine-gun fire, the *Leutnant* raced to another tank in order to issue orders and reports from there. In the meantime, the crew had assembled in a crater, where it applied field dressings to the badly wounded driver and the loader. Then there was no more dressing material. The second box of dressings was in the tank. Get up there one more time! It worked. We continued to apply more dressings. Everyone pitched in to help the driver. One of them still had his canteen, which he used to still the burning thirst of his comrade.

A few hundred meters off to the right, we saw light tanks advancing with riflemen. The *Leutnant* ran from the one tank across the open field and brought a fighting vehicle over to us. Then he ran off again in order to lead his company. The machine-gun fire had abated, so it was possible to get the driver and the three other wounded men on the tank, which then took them out of the fields of fire. We were able to transfer the gunner and the loader to the next available medic, who professionally applied dressings to them. We had to go farther back with the driver and the radio operator; every second was critical with them. The radio operator acted in a truly admirable manner. Despite his many wounds and being shot in the chest, he looked after the driver. An ambulance approached. It was stopped and, a few minutes later, the vehicle with the Red Cross was rolling back to the nearest main clearing station, where doctors and medics immediately tended to our two badly wounded men. They would have to stay in a field hospital for a few days, before they could be transported to the rear. The majority of the wounded, however, were already being taken to the nearest airfield that evening, where the *Ju 52's* were standing by to take the wounded comrades to hospitals in Germany.

When I went to the main clearing station the next day, I saw the radio operator lying in a rom. He had been lucky. A few ribs wounded. Although the shrapnel in the leg and the ribs hurt, his thoughts were more with his other comrades who were then rolling against the enemy. When I took off, he asked me to greet them for him.

THE HISTORY OF *PANZER-REGIMENT 6*

The regimental history[2] of *Panzer-Regiment 6* records the events of this chapter as follows:

On 10 July, the regiment (minus the 3rd Battalion, which remained in Rogatschew), was pulled out of the line and sent to the rear in the area around Brobruisk. It was intended to conduct an advance from there to the northeast along the major road to force a crossing over the Dnjepr and, correspondingly, through the "Stalin Line." To that end, the *3. Panzer-Division* was employed in the direction of Mogilew and the neighboring division, the *4. Panzer-Division*, towards Stary-Bychow. The lead *Kampfgruppe* was formed from *Schützen-Regiment 3* (*Oberst* von Manteuffel), reinforced by the 2nd Battalion of the tank regiment. That group received orders in the evening to force a crossing at Mogilew. Unfortunately, the division did not know that an infantry division had already tried in vain to take Mogilew from the west. That meant that the enemy had been warned.

Based on the recommendation of the commander of the 2nd Battalion (*Oberstleutnant* Munzel), the leader of the *Kampfgruppe* directed that tanks were to directly support the riflemen in their advance. Organization for combat: the 7th Company on the right with the battalion advancing on Buinitschi and the 5th Company on the left with *Kradschützen-Bataillon 3*. When the latter unit with its motorcycles was unable to get to the designated location for the attack on time due to the sandy routes, the company commander of the 5th Company, *Oberleutnant* Jarosch von Schweder, initially decided to advance on his own, since the terrain was open and not broken up.

Of all places, however, the area in question was the training area for the military facilities in Mogilew, and it had been secured in the nick of time by tank ditches and minefields. When the company moved out, it ran into those obstacles after about 100 meters and, in addition, received artillery and antitank-gun fire. Several tanks were immobilized, and the crews, who in some cases were only clad in bathing trunks due to the brutal heat, could only move back under the covering fire provided by other tanks. In the process, the commander's tank was also hit, and *Oberleutnant* von Schweder, along with his driver, *Gefreiter* Schnell, was mortally wounded. Eleven fighting vehicles were lost in that fight and were not able to be recovered until later.

---

2. Translator's Note: Munzel, *Gekämpft, gesiegt, verlosen,* 78.

The 8th Company, which was immediately send forward to provide relief, also ran into a minefield, causing the loss of additional tanks. In the meantime, the 7th Company fought with more success with the righthand battalion. Working closely with the riflemen, it was able to take the village of Buinitschi, the first suburb of Mogilew. In the process, it destroyed eight antitank guns and five tanks. But because the resistance continued to grow stronger, the division called off the attack.

The *4. Panzer-Division* succeeded in taking an intact wooden bridge at Stary-Bychow and forming a bridgehead over the Dnjepr. The *3. Panzer-Division* received orders to follow that division. Mogilew was not taken until later after days of fighting by a following infantry corps, while our armored corps had already advanced far east of the Dnjepr. In hindsight, the advance of Mogilew was undoubtedly too risky and would have probably not resulted in a crossing over the Dnjepr, since the enemy had been warned and offered strong resistance.

THE DIVISIONAL HISTORY

The divisional history[3] records the events of this chapter as follows:

The *3. Panzer-Division* had disengaged from its Dnjepr positions at Rogatschew with its last elements by 11 July 1941. It was located in a staging area south of Mogilew. There wasn't much time to rest, however. The free minutes were used to catch "forty winks," as long as the swarms of mosquitoes were not buzzing too wildly or smoked-out Russians didn't come running by.

At 1645 hours, the division formed a *Kampfgruppe* from elements of both brigades under the command of *Oberst* von Manteuffel, who received orders to attack Mogilew. The designated battalion and detachments moved further north until just before *Kradschützen-Bataillon 40* (*10. Infanterie-Division (mot.)*), which was in position there. The Russians were very active and were in the process of conducting an immediate counterattack against Nowaja Leschnewka. The *1./Schützen-Regiment 3* (*Oberleutnant* von Zitzewitz) was immediately employed against it. The riflemen advanced several kilometers to the north in their armored personnel carriers and were able to take Ssolanowka at 1930 hours.

At 1800 hours, *Generalleutnant* Model discussed the attack on Mogilew (population: 99,000) with his commanders.

---

3. Translator's Note: Traditionsverband, *Geschichte*, 130–31.

Kampfgruppe von Manteuffel moved into its designated staging areas. The *Oberst* placed his command post on the road 400 meters southwest of Mashissjadki. The commanders of the *II./Panzer-Regiment 6* (*Oberstleutnant* Munzel) and *Panzerjäger-Abteilung 521* (*Major* Frank) reported in there, as well as the commander of the 7th and 8th Companies of *Panzer-Regiment 6* and the commander of the headquarters company of *Schützen-Regiment 3*, whose company formed the reserve of the *Kampfgruppe*. The *6./Flak-Regiment 59* assumed area defense on both sides of Mashissjadki. The *1./Nachrichten-Abteilung 39* established radio communications with the forward elements of the division. During the day, *Pionier-Bataillon 39* employed all of its companies clearing the heavily mined terrain and completed its construction of a bridge over the Lechwa. The main clearing station was set up by both of the medical companies in Gluchaja-Seliba.

The *XXIV. Armee-Korps (mot.)* had the mission of forcing a crossing of the Dnjepr by using all of its forces. The attached divisions then attempted to execute that mission in the sectors assigned to them. In the course of that, the *3. Panzer-Division* was the left-wing division and it received a dual mission: protect the flank of the corps and take a good and armor-capable crossing point over the Dnjepr at Mogilew by rapidly taking it and its bridges.

During the night, *Artillerie-Regiment 75* brought its batteries into position, which initiated a short but intense preparation on the Soviet positions right at 0300 hours in the morning of 12 July. Shortly afterwards, the men of *Kampfgruppe von Manteuffel* moved out. The initial enemy resistance was broken, but then the difficulty of the terrain and the defensive preparedness of the strong enemy forces made itself felt.

The righthand group under *Major* Wellmann advanced northeast of Mashissjadki between the road and the railway line with the 2nd and 3rd Companies of *Schützen-Regiment 3*. Against expectations, both companies were able to quickly take the stopping point at Krassnitza and then move out on Sselez. The *3./Schützen-Regiment 3* took the meadowlands between the locality and the railway line, while the *2./Schützen-Regiment 3* stormed the village. Up to that point, the *7./Panzer-Regiment 6* and the *3./Pionier-Bataillon 39* had followed the riflemen. The tanks then took the lead, swung east, and reached a road running parallel to the river. They then bounded five kilometers north to Bunitschi in a single move. The Russians stubbornly defended the village and had employed their antitank guns in an especially skillful manner. Despite that, the fighting vehicles rolled through, destroying eight antitank guns and five tanks that crossed their paths. Then the attack bogged down. Fortunately, the first riflemen of the *2./Schützen-Regiment 3* then showed up and fought their way into and through the village, meter by meter. On the other hand, the *3./Schützen-Regiment 3* hung far back, since it was unable to eliminate enemy pockets of resistance that had been established on the railway northeast of Sselez. In fact, the Soviets launched an immediate counterattack there, which was able to be turned back with the assistance of the *1./Schützen-Regiment 3*, which was sent forward.

After noon, *Kampfgruppe Wellmann* made no progress anywhere. The enemy at Bunitschi turned active again and put a lot of pressure on the *2./Schützen-Regiment 3*, since Russian forces coming from the Dnjepr attacked the company in the flank. *Oberleutnant* von Baumbach was badly wounded and died a few hours later at the main clearing station. The *3./Schützen-Regiment 3* lost *Leutnants* Jobst and Haug through wounds. The battalion radioed the regiment that it was unable to advance anymore with its own forces and requested tanks and artillery immediately.

The lefthand *Kampfgruppe* under *Hauptmann* von Cochenhausen (*Kradschützen-Bataillon 3*, the *1./Schützen-Regiment 3*, the *5./Panzer-Regiment 6*, the *1./Panzerjäger-Abteilung 521*, and the *11./Schützen-regiment 3*) was also initially successful that morning. The tanks, riflemen, and antitank elements quickly gained ground west of the railway line, even though they had hardly any improved roads at their disposal. Tscheinowka was taken. The *5./Panzer-Regiment 6* advanced on its own in the open terrain west of the railway embankment. The first tank then flew into the air; a second one was also quickly immobilized. A third tank lost a track, with a fourth one sharing the same fate: mines. No matter where the fighting vehicles turned and moved, they ran over mines again and again and became immobilized. The crews were forced to bailed out, since the enemy placed well-aimed antitank-gun fire on the fighting vehicles. The Russian machine-gun and antitank-gun fire caused the company considerable casualties. *Oberleutnant* Jarosch von Schweder and *Gefreiter* Schnell were killed; many were wounded. In all, eleven fighting vehicles were lost. Although the remaining tanks provided covering fire, they had to disengage from the enemy. The crew of a knocked-out tank brought back *Leutnant* Hinzpeter, the new acting company commander. Thanks to its timely appearance, the *8./Panzer-Regiment 6*, which had been called forward, was able to give powerful support to the disengagement. It also lost a few vehicles, including the commander's tank, in the minefield. By noon, the 2nd Battalion had lost eighteen tanks, without making any further progress. As had been the case with the 1st Battalion at Schlobin, this was this battalion's "black day." Only the light platoon of the 2nd Battalion was able to make progress, advancing as far as Golynez, five kilometers west of Mogilew.

At that point, the division called off the unpromising attack on Mogilew.

The main clearing station in Sluzk.

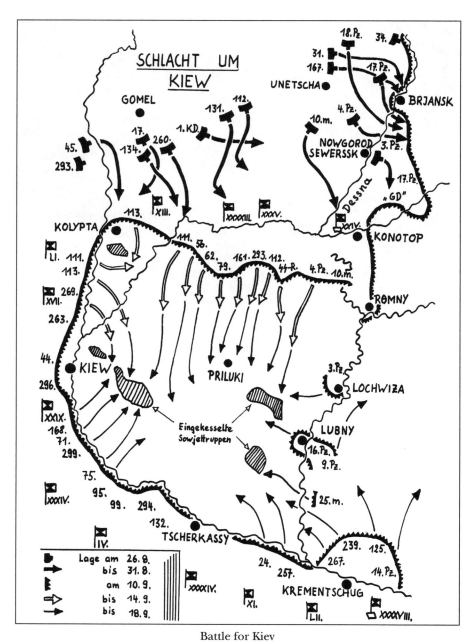

Battle for Kiev

Legend: *Lage am…* = Situation on … ; *bis* = until ; *Eingekesselte Sowjettruppen* = Encircled
Soviet forces.

CHAPTER 12

With *Cäsar* in Battle

**IN THE COMMAND TANK OF THE COMMANDING IN CHIEF
DURING THE ATTACK OF AN ARMORED DIVISION**

The woods filled with firs and spruce did not move. Even the smallest branch did not stir. The oppressive heat weighed down, unbearably muggy. Only the flies buzzed around us, restless, torturous spirits, and the crickets chirped away ceaselessly.

The wide woods of Soviet Russia had become our second homeland. We dwelled there, regardless of whether a general or a private. We drove . . . marched . . . fought . . . day and night in contact with the enemy. The earth was our bed. The small, camouflaged tent our house. Often enough, it was only a ditch or a foxhole. Then the high heavens were our blankets.

The command post of the commander in chief[1] moved from one patch of woods to the next. He was always in the middle of his corps and his divisions. At the moment, he moved with quick steps along the forest trail that had the small sign "Access Only for the Commander in Chief." He incorporated the willpower and the boldness of the German army field commander. There was always a confident smile on the weather-browned, fatherly face that all of the soldiers knew. Behind the thick hedge was a sleeping trailer. A low field cot in one part, a washbasin, and a narrow table. That was all there was, typical of a soldier. The chief of staff and the operations officer slept next to his trailer. At times when only the guards were still making their rounds, the commanding general frequently sat at that small table with the green waxed-cloth covering until the new morning dawned. It is there that he came up with his operations plans. Attack and breakthrough—again and again attack and breakthrough were

---

1. Translator's Note: This chapter concerns *Generaloberst* Guderian, the commander in chief of *Panzergruppe 2*, to which the *3. Panzer-Division* was attached during *Unternehmen "Barbarossa."*

his objectives. Before the enemy could establish himself, he had to be attacked.

The new order was at the corps. A masterpiece of military brevity and clarity. A single piece of typewriter paper, with double spacing between the individual paragraphs. Not a word too many, also not a word too little.

Tomorrow was another D-Day, where there would once again be a surprise thrust into the Bolshevik front. Armor and infantry formations would smash into the scattered enemy field armies in a combined attack; they would envelop and encircle them with a choke hold. Along the forest trails and along the roads, the tanks churned up dust among the marching infantry. Bareheaded, collars open, a scarf around the neck, the sleeves rolled high, the sun-browned faces covered in sweat and dirt, loaded down with a rifle or machine gun and ammunition, tired and yet still wide awake, they were the exact image of their fathers, who had marched along the long roads of Russia before them. Then, once again, it was August, just like twenty-seven years ago. The young soldiers were probably thinking about that.

The commander of the radio vehicle stood in front of the commander in chief.

"Which vehicle is it this time?"

"*Cäsar,*[2] *Herr Generaloberst.*"

The commander in chief smiled: "Then we'll most likely cross the Rubicon!"

There were a few more orders for the next day before we were released.

Cäsar was waiting in the concealment of a thicket. Its steel nose, on which its name was painted, protruded a bit. The soldiers showed no respect and referred to those types of armored vehicles as "bathtubs." It was the rolling field location of the commander in chief. It was only rarely that he was at his actual command post during the day. Whenever the attack was rolling, then he was always up front with his fighting and assaulting divisions and regiments. Through the wonder of radio, he was in constant contact with all of his commands. Regardless of whether the formations spread out or closed tight to form a pocket, whether they had to break through in separate wedges or suddenly form a hedgehog and defend, an intricate wireless network lay invisibly over them. The radioed orders of the commander in chief directed them. Like the

---

2. Translator's Note: Caesar.

radio transmission towers in front of a city, a "radio village" was located, hidden, at the edge of our command center containing the numerous stations of the command staffs. The radio village moved every few days. No precaution was neglected. Operations continued without a break. Perfect German technical capacity was the handmaiden of the art of war. The command tank, *Cäsar*, was the extended arm of that communications center.

The powerful engine rumbled quietly. Departure was ordered for 0400 hours. Exactly twelve hours later, the riflemen and infantrymen would head out for a new assault. The command tank had to be at its place then. The *Generaloberst* would not take off until first light in his *Kübelwagen*. With a single move, the vehicle commander jumped over the side wall. *"Panzer marsch!"* The heavens added an exclamation point to the command when they lit up with brilliant lightning and a powerful thunderclap. At the last minute, the crew was able to pull the weather cover over the thick antenna frame. Then the raging storm whipped down into the woods. Water shot down the narrow trails towards the meadowlands like a torrent. Everybody was happy to see this type of "ambush." The dusty lungs sucked down the fragrant aroma of the firs in mighty gulps. A steady rain, which softens up the already poor roads of the Soviet Union, is something to be feared. We had no use for that at all in this campaign. But that type of precipitation was refreshing. At least it held the terrible dust together for a short period. It goes without saying that the pelting drops lifted the spirits of the drivers. Happiest of all were the three motorcycle messengers who had to ride behind the command vehicle.

After half an hour, the storm was over. The *Leutnant* issued the order a second time: *"Panzer marsch!"* We rattled along the improved road for a while; it led south. The surface was asphalt. One of the few "show streets" that the Soviets had constructed besides their single vainglorious Minsk–Smolensk–Moscow Highway. We rolled across engineer bridges. The Bolsheviks had destroyed every river crossing in this sector as well. A recently dug-out tank ditch, filled with water, ran along both sides of the road. It had not been able to hold up the German fighting vehicles. The dull grumbling of thunder echoed our way.

The objective of the new German attack, which was aiming for deep in Soviet territory, was the roads leading to an important transportation hub.

Like the branches of a bolt of lightning, the *Kampfgruppen* of the armored formations advanced into the connecting roads of the area. It was there that the majority of the many encircled Bolshevik divisions defended especially toughly and stubbornly. The trails, roads, and woods between the armor avenues of approach remained stubbornly in the possession of the Soviets until their encircled elements were rubbed out and destroyed. Those dangerous islands of resistance of the Bolsheviks were eliminated by the infantry formations. While the assaulting rifle regiments of a motorized infantry division assaulted the city of Smolensk on 16 July, the encircled Soviet elements had already been defending for days. But their fate would soon be sealed.

The terrain, in which the fighting was then being conducted, had changed. The thinly populated wood and marshland of White Ruthenia, with its unproductive fields, was weeks behind us. The fields in this area were richer and bore more fruit. In the meantime, the grain had ripened. Broad expanses glistened a golden yellow in the evening sun. The large potato fields bloomed white and lavender.

Up to then, the war in the East had shown no mercy. Many villages were along the way from which only a couple of burned chimneys remained. Gruesomely savaged cities over which the smell of pestilence hung. Around this location, the torch had spared a few villages. But only women and old men stood in front of the houses and looked at the endless columns rolling past. The men had all been called up by the Soviets. Whoever could no longer carry a rifle was forced to work on fortifications. They did that for 100 grams of bread a day, if they received anything at all, prisoners told us.

We overtook a battery of assault guns. The cannoneers were sitting happily on their squat tracked vehicles, some of which show the scars of battle. As a unit symbol, they had a charging elephant. With their thick armor and short, powerful main guns, they reminded one of war elephants turned into machines. The soldiers stretched their necks in vain to see the commander in chief, since they recognized his command vehicle despite the hidden commander's pennant. It was a nice ride, since even the tracks, which usually tossed the dust in the air like dredgers, rolled without causing any dust that day. But the road . . . that devilish, blasted rolling roadway in the Soviet Union! You wouldn't want to believe that a tracked vehicle would be tossed about like a wheeled one on those crater-filled pathways. Think again! It was like a maritime journey at high seas. The armored vehicle was shaken back and forth.

It was an art form to steer the heavy vehicle past the columns when going forty to fifty kilometers an hour. More so the achievement of radioing and writing reports in a clear and legible manner so that the commander in chief could read them.

When marching like that, you are happy about every kilometer you can put behind you. But one of the many tributaries of the Dnjepr outside the next large village upset the apple cart. The vehicles had already halted in long columns. A wooden bridge had collapsed under the heavy loads. Although the engineers were already on the scene, new pilings had to be rammed in. That would last until at least the next morning. God knows, this campaign has had its share of those types of small surprises.

The motorcycle messengers raced off to find a detour or a ford. A bridge was found a few kilometers away, but as soon as a light truck moved across it, it started to sway dangerously. It was capable of three tons, at the most. We had to return to the old road. An impressive night march past rolling columns started.

The next morning, the fireball of the sun rose blood red behind the dark woods. At that moment, *Stukas* thundered above us and off into the distance. They provided the signal for the attack. We looked at our watches; it was exactly 0400 hours. The assault was starting!

In a wide semicircle around our avenue of advance heading south, the German guns roared out their brazen language of destruction on that August morning. Their hail of steel hammered onto the grain fields and patches of woods, where the trenches and dugouts of the Bolshevik infantry and the firing positions of their batteries had been identified. The seasoned assault soldiers ran forward under the cover of the wall of fire: carbines, submachine guns, and hand grenades in hard fists. Reconnaissance aircraft and aerial artillery observers circled over the front. We were in the western portion of the large attack wave. It was terrain with long, extended swells in the ground. Rye fields intermingled with meadows and woods. It was difficult for the infantry to cross through it. In the next village after the river was the headquarters of a Berlin-Brandenburg armored division. *Cäsar* was to wait there for the commander in chief. The earth was as dry as a bone again. The usual flags of sand signaled the approach routes. They were also the targets of Bolshevik artillery. The fountains of dreck sprang high all around. We ducked low behind the steel walls of *Cäsar* as we raced through it.

But the rounds were also hammering into the village where the command post was located. It was on a slight rise and was certainly visible from the opposite swell in the ground. Three muffled reports—everyone counted along: 1, 2, 3—then the rounds howled and whistled their way towards us. Shrapnel yelped, swirled and sang all around us. The radio vehicle moved along the protective wall of a long barn. The riflemen had dug out fresh foxholes there prior to the assault on the next rye field. Scattered everywhere were the *Kübelwagen* of the headquarters, the signals vehicles, and the radio command vehicles. The operations officer had spread out a command map on a quickly procured wooden table in front of one of the log houses. To his side were the usual assistants, the liaison officers of the regiments and the *Luftwaffe*, signals officers, messengers, and motorcyclists.

Of course, it was impossible to work under that artillery fire. The impacts were landing too closely to the village and the surrounding houses. Only the radio operators sat with their headphones, Morse key in their hands, in their vehicles and at their stations.[3] All of us had to get into the shrapnel dugouts as quickly as possible. The three guns and the other batteries that were spraying the assault gun to our right were a weak artillery defense seen from the big picture, but for us soldiers who were in the middle of the witch's cauldron, those were intense periods.

"The main thing is that nothing happens to *Cäsar!*" the *Unteroffizier* said behind the steel wall. It was the only thing the crew was worried about.

The Bolsheviks placed round after round into the village. The rounds tore fist-size chunks out of the wood-beamed walls. After we heard the third report of the guns firing, we all ducked down with expectant faces, like nodding Buddhas.

We then smiled when the shrapnel zinged past us after the impacts. A round then crashed directly into the barn with the straw-thatched roof fifty meters from us. The roof caught fire and the whole thing immediately blazed up, all of the wooden construction. A worried question: Was our outbuilding endangered by the swirling sparks? Fortunately, the wind

---

3. Translator's Note: While radio traffic at regimental level and below was generally voice, higher commands usually used Morse code to transmit messages, thus requiring higher-level radio operators to be school-trained.

drove the flames in the opposite direction. German batteries then engaged the Bolshevik guns. They increased their fire. We liked the sound of our guns better. Then there were only individual, scattered impacts. Finally, they also stopped. The Bolshevik guns had been silenced. The radio report from the German artillery battalion arrived: "Enemy battery eliminated!" That's the way it had been in all previous attacks. Along the Beresina and along the Dnjepr. In a cannon duel, the German guns always emerged victorious.

Increased activity at the command post. The reports flowed in from all sides via wire and radio. Motorcycle messengers hurtled in, the report forms pressed between their lips so that they didn't fly away. At the same time, it was the best ticket to pass all obstacles. The picture on the map changed constantly. The riflemen and the tanks fought their way forward. Kilometer by kilometer, the arrows and arcs worked their way towards the objective. But it was another difficult assault. The Bolsheviks had dug in once again—in the furrows of the potato fields, in the rye, in the ditches along the roads, beneath vegetation and trees, everywhere. Lately, they had started using narrow, smaller dugouts in the ground to protect themselves better against artillery impacts. The Russian soldier was the first one to learn to wield the shovel. The Bolsheviks also understood how to do so with great skill. The next village was hotly contested. Apparently, one of the few good infantry regiments was there, and it put up a tough defense. The newly assembled units generally only offered weak resistance. The Germany artillery slammed into the Bolshevik positions. One fiery torch after the other climbed skyward; the village turned into a single sea of flame. The riflemen immediately attacked through it. Another entry on the map.

The enemy positions were quickly broken through at all locations. The surviving Bolsheviks came out of the holes and trenches with raised hands and fear-etched faces. They were sent to the rear in groups. The artillery reported it was changing positions forward. The division command post was also moved forward.

We were moving forward! The columns started to move. With them was the radio command vehicle *Cäsar*. The two radio operators and their *Unteroffizier* sat on the side walls. A professional, an electrical worker by trade. The "radio village" started calling. The first reports from the command staffs. A tangle of letters was sent and received. The alphabet arbitrarily and purposely tangled together several thousand times.[4] Whether the tank bounces like a donkey on a bad road or is slung about like a boat at sea, whether the sun shines or only the green light of a flashlight bestows the minimum light necessary at night, whether in the front lines or in the quiet of a wooded reserve—none of that concerns the radio operator. For him, there are only dots and dashes in the air. The reports have to been written in a clearly legible manner. They had to train a lot before they became a cohesive team that nothing shakes up. Radio operators are not allowed to have nerves. Telephone operators and radio operators are also combat troops. With their great service, they have contributed to the success of this campaign. They've also lost a few comrades in combat.

The corps staffs move forward with the divisions. One village name after the other appears in the radio traffic. The map clearly showed the progress of the enveloping attack. The net grew ever tighter. The reconnaissance aircraft constantly reported the front-line trace. We move through burning, smoky villages . . . through depressions . . . across high ground. Large circles look like they had been shaved into the fields of rye. The destructive fires of the German artillery on the Bolsheviks, who had hidden themselves there. Engineers had tough work ahead of them again. Short stretches of corduroy roads and patched-together crossing points made marshy routes negotiable. The sun burned glowing hot. You could see rolling march groups on all of the roads, artillery and *Flak*. Despite dust and sweat, you could see high morale on the faces of the soldiers, just as you always do in a war of movement.

A big jump forward. The command post set up in a fir forest. The soldiers set about camouflaging the vehicles and digging emplacements. The *Flak* pulled into the new position. For the first time that day, Bolshevik bombers attacked. Nine machines approached from the blinding rays of the sun. Their aluminum bodies shone metallic white—Martin bombers. They dropped their bombs, accompanied by the bark of the *Flak*. Everybody flattened out on the ground and the moss. There was a howling and whooshing next to us that grew louder, at the spot where

---

4. Translator's Note: The author is referring to the operation of the top-secret "Enigma" encryption device. Unbeknownst to the Germans, the Poles had broken the code before the war started and gave the codes to the British at the start of the war, thus compromising the entire German message-traffic network.

the division commander had just dismounted from his vehicle. Everyone's senses were at the breaking point. A few hundred meters farther, black clouds of smoke from crashing impacts climbed over the crowns of the trees. Comrades hurried in that direction; medics were alerted; a few dead and wounded were sustained. Fighters came rocketing up. The caught the Soviet machines. It goes without saying that a few Ratas, Soviet fighters, attempted to strafe as well. As a precautionary measure, the vehicle commander had the antiaircraft sight placed on the machine gun on *Cäsar*. But the Soviet fighters only made two runs. The impacts of the machine-gun rounds struck the ground a few meters from the vehicle.

The *Generaloberst* arrived at the command post of our armored division a short while later. Covered in dust, like everyone else. His adjutant looked like he had just arrived from the middle of the Libyan Desert. The commander in chief had been on the go since the start of the attack. While the *Generaloberst* read the reports, his adjutant made a few amusing comments in his Berlin dialect.[5] One of the secrets of the success of our army is the heartfelt relationship between the officers of all ranks and the simple soldiers, a relationship that exists in no other army of the world.

In the *Cäsar*, the key strokes on the encryption device never stopped. The orders sailed through the ether. The infantry fought its way forward through the woods, meadows, fields, and marshland. Armored formations thrust into withdrawing enemy. Their command posts were our next objective. The voice radios were turned on. Even while moving, the commander in chief or his signals officers stayed in constant contact with our vehicle commander. It was an amazing experience to be able to ride along in that wandering command post for the attack operation.

In the vicinity of the corps command post was the first prisoner collection point. The Bolsheviks always reminded you of feral beings—under the whip of the commissars, a violence-prone, ill-disciplined band of soldiers, which was not afraid of any type of brutality or barbarism. Liberated from the pressure of those torturers, happy to be out from under the hell of the German artillery and the *Stukas*, they made the impression that they were incapable of committing even the smallest act of indecency. The fear of being mown down by friendly machine guns at their backs and the threat that they would be executed while in German

---

5. Translator's Note: Germans from Berlin are famous for their sharp tongues and wit within the rest of Germany.

captivity are the driving forces behind their frequent tough resistance. There were no officers among them, as the translators determined. They were painfully avoiding every recognizable external insignia. Even in the facial expressions, there was seldom a difference. Only the higher command levels still wore their rank. The officers were the first ones to flee, the prisoners said.

The interrogation of those prisoners, even in a large group, confirmed the fact that the Bolshevik field armies had been defeated. There were soldiers from three infantry regiments there, which had been formed from the remnants of seven different regiments. Each of the wiped-out regiments had previously belonged to a different division. Some of the prisoners had only received rudimentary training. Many were raw recruits. The heavy loss of weapons had had an effect. Airborne forces had been employed that had to be brought forward by foot march. Transport aircraft had been missing for a long time. Artillery regiments had been identified that had no guns; there were barely enough rifles for the gunners.

The translators interrogated the artillerymen in a segregated group. The same impression. A new artillery regiment had been formed from three different regiments. Despite that, it only had incomplete batteries. It slowly dawned on the primitive minds of the prisoners how shamefully and disgracefully they had been deceived and lied to by those in power. Despite all that, it may not be underestimated how those soldiers, no matter how much they may or may not believe their lives had been forfeited, continued to be tough, stubborn fighters, who often had to be beaten to death in their trenches, because they did not want to surrender. Every gun, every machine gun, every mortar, and every foxhole had to be brought down and taken. The hard fight continued; it continued to demand the greatest heroism of our soldiers.

A captured division commander was brought in for interrogation. A division commissar from another division was also brought in. The latter held the rank of a colonel, according to him. Deprived of his outward signs of power—he had removed the large Red Stars on the uniform sleeves, and the rank patches from the red collar tabs were in his pocket— he was only one of many who had given up the game.

He sat in the roadside ditch, crestfallen. He stared in a fixed manner at the seemingly endless band of prisoners who trotted by, tired and tarnished. He was thirty-nine; he only knew Bolshevism. His world had collapsed, much like the hollow and fragile plaster statues of Lenin and Stalin in the marketplaces of the impoverished and burned-down villages.

On the other side of the road, German infantry was marching and guns jolted along behind horses into the city. The secured the area that had just been taken. The armored formations had advanced 900 kilometers between Brest-Litowsk and Smolensk, fighting and attacking the entire way. The new thrust led another 100 kilometers farther. The infantry regiments had marched 1,000 kilometers on Russia's roads, on secondary routes through broad forests, on narrow pathways through meadowlands and swamps, under a glowing sun and streaming rain. Behind them were battles, engagements, and the last few difficult days of assaults. But the glow of victory was on their faces. Where was Brandenburg? Where was Berlin? Sixteen hundred, perhaps even seventeen hundred kilometers distant. They sang. *Weit ist der Weg zurück ins Heimatland . . .*[6] Their march continued eastward. It was the route all were taking. Until final victory!

The discussions of the commander in chief with the commanding generals were over. Evening twilight sank over the first day of attack. We moved back into "orders city" in the woods.

The fast *Kübelwagen* took off. There was still work waiting at the command post. Preceding the commander in chief, the final radioed orders flew through the ether. *Cäsar* rattled all by itself through the night. Hour after hour, only the light, bumpy ribbon of sand and the streaming moon were our escorts. It was not until the bright morning that the radio vehicle once more pushed itself under the concealment of the spruces and firs, exactly thirty-six hours later. The sun was already bright and high on the firmament and the birds sang and twittered, as we crawled into our tents, dead tired. The crew of another radio vehicle was already alert. It would soon rattle down the wooded path. We were sleeping so soundly we didn't hear it.

THE HISTORY OF *PANZER-REGIMENT 6*

The regimental history[7] of *Panzer-Regiment 6* records the events of this chapter as follows:

The attack started at 0400 hours. It was initiated by *Stukas* and initially made rapid progress. Thanks to the industry of the maintenance company,

---

6. Translator's Note: "The road is far leading back home"
7. Translator's Note: Munzel, *Gekämpft, gesiegt, verloren,* 81.

the regiment had 103 tanks operational. The 1st Battalion advanced on the left, the 3rd Battalion on the right, and the 2nd Battalion behind and approximately in the middle. Mikulitschi, twenty-five kilometers distant, was taken in the afternoon. A bridgehead was immediately established across the Oster River. The bridgehead was largely the result of the actions of *Oberleutnant* Vopel, whose 1st Company took three bridges within ten minutes, even though two of them were defended by artillery. All were captured intact. The 1st Battalion immediately followed, with the 2nd Battalion right behind it. Both of the battalions advanced together with von Manteuffel's rifle regiment and threw the enemy back to behind the railway line leading to Roslawl. Prior to moving out, *Generaloberst* Guderian, our field army commander, appeared and praised the regiment. He was also extensively briefed on the cause of the previous losses of fighting vehicles.

THE DIVISIONAL HISTORY

The divisional history[8] records the events of this chapter as follows:

The 1st of August 1941 promised to be another sunny and warm day. Punctually, starting at 0345 hours, *Artillerie-Regiment 75* fired with all of its tubes on the enemy positions. The German attack was underway! Tanks and personnel carriers rattled through meadows, blooming canola fields and through the burning, squalid villages. The entire *3. Panzer-Division* was advancing after the *I./Schützen-Regiment 3*, which was screening from its old positions until the morning, was relieved by *Schützen-Regiment 33* (*4. Panzer-Division*). Once again, *Generalleutnant* Model found himself in the midst of his advancing soldiers. He ordered his command post in Goljejewka, which was still under enemy artillery fire, to prepare to move at 0645 hours.

The morning sun streamed over the wide land. The enemy fought toughly. His defense focused around the small village of Bednja on dominant high ground. After a short artillery preparation, the *I./Panzer-Regiment 6* (*Oberstleutnant* Schmidt-Ott) attacked the village from the west and the south at the same time, capturing it. The division commander arrived with the first riflemen, had the men immediately mount up on the fighting vehicles, and ordered a continuation of the attack.

---

8. Translator's Note: Traditionsverband, *Geschichte*, 142–43.

The mood improved by the hour. The men were advancing again! *Panzer-Regiment 6* started the new offensive with 103 fighting vehicles: 37 *Panzer II's*, 42 *Panzer III's*, 16 *Panzer IV's*, and 8 command tanks. That was exactly half the amount of tanks that crossed the frontier on 22 June. The leading attack columns of the two *Kampfgruppen* linked up shortly after 0800 hours at the bridge over the Ssoshenka in Wabitschewka. By doing so, the first attack objective had been reached. *Oberstleutnant* Audörsch then took over the lead elements and pressed on to the northeast against Studenez with *Schützen-Regiment 394* and the *I./Panzer-Regiment 6*. The enemy defended there; he knew that the strongpoint prevented the crossing of the German formations over the Oster. *Kradschützen-Bataillon 3* (*Major* von Corvin-Witzbitzki) determined that the village was occupied, but that did not deter him from advancing. He pivoted his companies to the southeast. The *I./Schützen-Regiment 3* (*Major* Wellmann) was employed against the village. By 1200 hours, the *2./Schützen-Regiment 3* had taken the village, establishing outposts oriented to the east.

By then, the main body of the division had advanced along the roads leading southeast from Studenez and pressed into the wooded terrain in front of the river. *Generalleutnant* Model directed the attack from Studenez; *Major i.G.* Pomtow and the battle staff had followed him there.

The next objective for the division was Mikulitschi. Both of the *Kampfgruppen* formed advance guards that were then set in march in the direction of the river along the two roads. The first units to reach the city were the *1./Panzer-Regiment 6* of *Oberleutnant* Vopel and the *3./Pionier-Bataillon 39* under *Leutnant* Schultze. The fighting vehicles disregarded the enemy outposts and advanced right into Mikulitschi, soon positioned in front of the first bridge, which they took. The Russians had brought two long-barreled cannon into position at the second bridge, but they were so surprised by the lightning-fast appearance of the tanks that they were unable to get off a round. Machine-gun fire and high-explosive rounds kept the crews low. While the fighting vehicles continued to roll, *Oberstleutnant* Audörsch appeared with the *1./Schützen-Regiment 394* and elements of the engineer battalion. The riflemen and engineers jumped to the ground and drove off the bridge guards, who had wanted to pour fuel on the structure. They captured the bridge. A short while later, another defended bridge was taken by the *1./Panzer-Regiment 6* and the riflemen of *Schützen-Regiment 394*. *Leutnant* Möllhoff (the *2./Pionier-Bataillon 39*) contributed magnificently to the operation and later received a by-name mention in the Army Honor Roll. The first bridgehead over the Oster was formed in the shortest time imaginable by the assaults of all of the forces employed in that area.

Generaloberst Guderian and *Generalleutnant* Model arrived up front at the same time at Mikulitschi. They both moved forward into the bridgehead and praised the participating tankers and riflemen. As a result of the rapid taking of the bridgehead, a new situation had developed, causing the entire *3. Panzer-Division* to be brought forward into the bridgehead, even though enemy forces still existed in the woods north of the river. According to prisoner statements, for example, there were strong forces in the woods between Chawrotowka and Mikulitschi, including a corps headquarters. Based on that, the *I./Schützen-Regiment 3*, *Panzerjäger-Abteilung 543* and the *9./Panzer-regiment 6* surrounded the woods in order to clear out the Soviets in the morning.

CHAPTER 13

The Secretive Patch of Woods

IN THE COMMAND CENTER UNDER THE TREES IN THE VICINITY OF SMOLENSK

In the life of a soldier, woods play an important role. Especially in the broad expanse of Russia, the concealment provided by nature offers cover against exposure from the ground and the air. In Russia, there is no lack of forests. Our little patch of woods with the high deciduous trees was a little bit off the beaten path. It was the old postal road to Smolensk, which was bearing the proud name of an "armor avenue of advance" at the time. It was neither better nor worse than all of the horrific roads in Russia. Day by day, the innumerable holes and bumps were expanded ever deeper. In the case of a cloudburst or a storm, they were transformed in the blink of an eye into a muddy, slimy one-way route. In the penetrating heat of July, they dried out quickly. Everything disappeared in their swirling clouds of dust. The tortured vehicles conducted a wild, out-of-control dance on them. The drivers, who were concerned about the suspension and axles, cursed in every type of dialect imaginable. The same way Napoleon's carriage and horse riders might have cursed.

The roads were hotly contested. After all, they headed directly into the depths of the fortified "Stalin Line" behind the Dnjepr. We saw the same scene that we had frequently seen before. Shot-up and burned-out tanks, in some cases right behind freshly excavated tank ditches; knocked-out batteries in great number. They were the milestones of the German victory march everywhere. Piece by piece, the powerful Soviet armaments were being dismantled. Fighting demanded sacrifice. Correspondingly, there were also the small plots of consecrated ground. Their crosses, frequently formed out of the brilliant white of birch trees, demonstrated the offensive sprit and heroic deaths in the big battle for Smolensk. Resting in the middle of this road among comrades and a single tree was the young

Leutnant Keitel, the son of the *Generalfeldmarschall*. In that difficult battle for freedom against Jewish world Bolshevism, all circles of society within the German people contributed their pure sacrifice of blood for the perpetual existence of the *Reich*. Fathers and sons, mothers and women, brothers and sisters—as it has been for centuries.

A command flag pointed towards the narrow field path, heading down the patch of woods in the open bottomland. At first glace, the patch of woods seemed no different than thousands of others. Then one discovered a chain of small ponds. That was most welcome. In that savage heat, you greeted every opportunity to wash and to bathe. As long as you had time to do so. A small village was beyond the ponds. Most of the wooden houses had been burned down to the ground. Among the ashes, carbonized beams, and black flecks left by fire, there was a large, white ruins comprised of stone. It was oddly strange and foreign in this unpopulated and melancholy landscape. It was a crumbling church. Its roof had collapsed. That had been years ago. Its stonework had aged. Grass and weeds grew among the rubble. It was most certainly the possession of a Russian landowner, before the Bolsheviks had set the house and holdings alight and blew the chapel sky high.

One of the many pockets of enemy resistance which formed the "Stalin Line" beyond the Dnjepr around Smolensk extended around the village and the ruins. The observation post of their artillery had been located in an improvisational manner behind the boards placed to reinforce the remnants of the steeple. The riflemen had sat behind holes in the wall and piles of rubble with their machine guns and automatic weapons. German pilots had smoked out the positions with well-aimed bombs. Bomb and artillery craters were located close together. Tin roofs were the only sign that outbuildings had once been there. They were riddled with tracer ammunition from on-board weapons. Perhaps the patch of woods had been a park at one time, with the fishponds of the estate. That could no longer be determined. Twenty years of decay and neglect were a long time. Skillfully emplaced Soviet positions were positioned along the edge of the woods, along the field paths, and along the bodies of water. Dugouts for antitank guns and heavy machine guns, foxholes with camouflaged rifle ports, sections of grass placed back over the dug-out earth. We pitched our tents next to them. It saved some work in having to dig shrapnel trenches. Prisoners of war were already employed in burying the unbearably sweet stinking animal cadavers. Orphaned calves and lambs were caught. Fresh meat for the troops. Those are the laws of war.

The war deprived that small patch of woods some of its tranquility for a short time. *Generaloberst* Guderian established his command post there under the leaves and pine needles.

High headquarters are more difficult to accommodate than entire infantry regiments. The patch of woods was filled to the brim with vehicles. All of the vehicles were camouflaged with branches, vegetation, and small trees. That was necessary. Occasionally, a Soviet reconnaissance aircraft or a Red fighter skimmed quickly above the terrain, since the front was not too far away. Just a few kilometers to the north, the Dnjepr twisted and turned parallel to the road. The artillery positions and field fortifications of the Bolsheviks were on the other side. They sat encircled in the long narrow "tube" between the two armored corps that had broken through between the river, the railway line, and the large highway (the latter two leading to Moscow). The Bolsheviks attempted over and over again to free themselves from the encirclement in increasingly desperate breakout attempts. They could see a portion of the road from the jutting bend in the Dnjepr. Harassment fire from individual guns was constantly being placed there. Smolensk continued to be engaged as well—rounds from heavy-caliber guns, probably from a 21-centimeter railway gun, which moved back and forth along tracks in the "tube." During the night, a glowing red semicircle lit up the sky over the city.

The command staff of the commander in chief is a small city on wheels. A masterpiece the way it had disappeared in the patch of woods, divided into administrative sections with their own streets and pathways. There were the small guidepost signs everywhere in the trees with their tactical symbols and the mysterious abbreviations. Like the German armed forces in general, we also found a marvel of German organizational ability on a smaller scale there. All created for the single purpose of allowing the commander in chief to lead his mobile forces. It was clear that this war in the East was being conducted with all combat arms and technical means of support. For that reason, all of the combat, combat support, and combat service support branches were represented at the command post of the *Panzergruppe*. It goes without saying that the individual commanders had their own staffs with adjutants, liaison officers, clerks, and messengers as well. All of it was a finely tuned machine, representing years of experience. One cog meshed with the next.

Every city has its city hall in the middle of it with a large plaza. In this case, it was the actual command post of the *Generaloberst*, his command vehicle, and the work bus of the staff. A large area was cordoned off by tape. Military police guards kept vehicles away. It goes without saying that there had to be silence around the work desk of the commander in chief. The war knew no interruption. Even on days of apparent quiet, there was ceaseless work on operations plans. The *Generaloberst* sat at a small, wobbly desk in front of a large map under a shady tree. Around his neck was the Knight's Cross of the Iron Cross with Oak Leaves, which the chief adjutant of the *Führer* had brought the previous day. His closest associates sat across from him. It was there that the big operations plans were executed and the tactical orders issued. The assistants of the General Staff officers worked in the bus; adjutants and liaison officers came and went. One telephone conversation followed the previous one. Reports were received; new orders issued. The divisions of the armor corps were in difficult fighting against a bitterly defending enemy.

The weather-browned face of the *Generaloberst* was serious and contemplative. His sentences concerning the new attack were short and to the point. Only a few words were necessary among the three men used to working together. The two fists of the commander in chief lay firmly on the table, causing the knuckles to turn white, while he spoke about the blue ribbon of the Dnjepr. Then he suddenly spread out his fingers. They seemed to be following the objectives of his armored corps and divisions, as if he wanted to thrust through the new Soviet line of resistance. A symbolic meaning lay in that small, energy-filled gesture. That was the way it had been in Poland and also in France, when the armor general thrust across the Sedan to the English Channel. They were once again fists in a steel enclosure when they punched through the Bolshevik resistance at the Bug, the Beresina, and the Dnjepr with armored fingers continuously pushing their way forward forcefully. But between the fingers, just as it was with the motorized and armored divisions, the Bolshevik field armies and corps remained behind—broken apart, torn to pieces, without lines of communication or unified command. Until the fingers closed again. There was no escape from their encirclement, only death or captivity. With a powerful hand, the commander in chief marked lines, arrows, and circles on the map. The battle for Smolensk was still underway. The Bolsheviks had identified the danger of a deadly thrust into the heartland of the Soviet Union. Soviet Marshal Timoshenko committed ever more reserves into the German flank so as to take back Smolensk, the "gateway into the greater Russian heartland." But the final kilometers drew inexorably closer and constricted the "tube" around Smolensk. But the *Generaloberst* was already well beyond Smolensk. He had already thought through his next attack. The orders had already been issued.

Commanders of field armies have to be artists. There is a reason why one speaks of the art of war. Every war has its own face. The area and the enemy provide the characteristics. The noteworthy difficulties of this campaign could clearly be seen on that command map. The wedges and pockets were dominant. One could see how the armored corps had thrust far ahead of the infantry divisions into the Soviet field army, literally without looking to the left or the right. Two days after the storming of Smolensk, other motorized divisions were out another seventy-five kilometers, forming a strong bridgehead at Jelnja in the middle of the Red flood. The flanks became ever longer, frequently only screened by weak forces. In place of a large encirclement, there were numerous pockets and sacks. In that land of limited roadways and terrain blocked by waterways, envelopment was only possible along the few roads.

Of course, that meant combat leadership at an intense level, coupled with great danger. Only masterful leadership and an excellently armed and trained force could conduct that type of warfare and win it. Crises were unavoidable. The strong Bolshevik forces attempted to break out of those pockets, using the fires of their large numbers of artillery and under the cover of their many tanks. Part of the bargain was the occasional heavy blow to the flanks or the constant endangerment to the long logistics lines of communication. It had to be assumed that some armored divisions would be cut off. They formed a hedgehog and defended until relief forces could clear a way to them. There was no doubt that the Soviet leadership intended to cut off the far-ranging armored corps from the following infantry divisions. But they lacked the forces for that at the moment. The armored wedges had broken the back of the Soviet field armies in the first rush. The field armies that followed completed the work of destruction. New arrows pushed forward constantly on the command map. Like the shaft following the tip of the spear. Those were the infantry divisions, which were brought forward in forced marches. The "queen of battle" had performed magnificently. From the General Governorate to Smolensk by foot! In some cases, accompanied by difficult fighting. They had to comb the woods and, in some places, take the Dnjepr for a second time. For four weeks, a daily march performance of thirty-five kilometers— that was our infantry! The wedge had spread out to form a new front. Until the armored fists struck again.

The conference was over. The *Kübelwagen* and the radio vehicle of the *Generaloberst* had moved forward. For a moment, the commander in chief looked over the broad land with his bright eyes. A fresh breeze of air rushed through the trees. Black storm clouds approached. The small column started to move out.

Just like the radio waves bridged the gaps between the armored wedges, the weapons and bombs of the *Luftwaffe* dominated the enemy in front of, next to, and behind the armored divisions. Worthy of admiration in this campaign, as in the ones before it, was their self-sacrificing brotherhood-in-arms. It was only as a result of their assistance and their never-ending operations that the bold war of pockets and wedges was possible. They screened the breakthrough and prevented surprises. Moving past this group of woods, the flights, squadrons, and groups of *Stukas*, heavy bombers, and bomb-laden destroyers droned by. It was always a magnificent sight for the soldiers on the ground, whenever the heavily laden birds flew in closed formation towards the enemy, looking like a parade above the East-West Axis in Berlin.

During the night, when the first shimmer of morning started to appear, the deep rumble of engines could be heard right above the patch of woods. That could only be a Soviet aircraft, one of those multi-engine, slow-flying crates, which were only employed by the Bolsheviks at night. The noise died out, only to become louder and stronger and then to fade again. The pilot was circling and looking. Did he intend to attack the command post? Had the reconnaissance aircraft that afternoon actually discovered the secretive woods. An antiaircraft machine gun fired in long bursts. That meant that our forward outposts had taken the machine under fire. There were rifle rounds in between. Quite close. The report soon arrived that the machine had gone down a kilometer away. Soldiers ran towards it from all sides. It was one of those large four-engine transport machines with a large protruding glass canopy that had landed in the field. It was loaded with seven sacks full of infantry ammunition. The crew had taken off across the cornfield. A noncommissioned officer remained behind with a round in the thigh. As was later determined, he was a gunner. A second man was located during the search in the field. Two more were killed in machine-gun fire. The other five, including the pilot-in-charge and the officers, were able to escape in the corn and vegetation. Despite an energetic search, they were not found.

The two prisoners were brought in for interrogation. It had been intended for the transporter to bring in ammunition for the encircled Bolshevik forces. But ground fog and low-lying cloud cover had made the drop impossible. Upon its return, the machine had gotten completely lost. When the first machine-gun bullets hit the tail and the wings, the pilot-in-charge probably thought that he was being engaged by Soviet soldiers. He landed in order to identify himself. Of course, the two didn't want to let on completely. Everything had happened as fast as lightning. Fear still flickered in their eyes. As was often the case during interrogations with airmen, their first question was whether they were going to be shot. Despite all assurances to the contrary, they probably continued to fear that they were going to be "drawn and quartered" after the interrogation, as their officers and commissars had drilled into their heads. You could see it in them. They knew very little of the general war situation. Officially, news about the war was only relayed to them by the *Politruk*, the political commissar, who regurgitated radio reports. On the sly, however, the news of the taking of Smolensk had filtered through. The morale of the forces was bad. The large casualties among aircrews and losses in aircraft could not be kept quiet, of course. The *Politruk* maintained a reign of terror. Every Soviet airman believed that the Germans killed all prisoners, especially aviators. That was the only reason the remaining aircrew had fled. When the two prisoners were led off, the unwounded man looked around fearfully. "We're not going to shoot you!" the interpreter called out after him in Russian.

In the area around Smolensk, the Russian command attempted one more time to break through into the flanks of the German armored corps by the introduction of new reserves and relieve the pocket. Soviet forces pressed into the northern portion of Smolensk. They advanced in the deep valley of the Dnjepr; they were turned back with bloody losses. For days on end, one armored corps fought far out in front at the Jelnja bridgehead along the railway line into Smolensk. The Bolsheviks drove forward new and strong waves of forces again and again from the north, the east, and the south. One of those tank attacks penetrated to the eastern outskirts of the city, until it collapsed in the face of the combined antitank and *Flak* fires. In two days, seventy-eight tanks were destroyed, including eight fifty-two-ton steel monsters. They charged the German positions for ten days. The dead were literally piled high into mountains in front of some of the German positions. The German defenders almost ran out of ammunition. As was often the case, Junkers transporters dragged in rounds and belts of machine-gun ammunition. The *Stukas* and bombers flew mission after mission. Choking in blood, all of the Bolshevik attacks bogged down. Jelnja, the German bridgehead, remained firmly in the hands of the armor corps until the infantry divisions had closed in. That signaled the final decision in the Battle of Smolensk.

The trains, the maintenance facilities, and the supply services constantly do their best. Here: Issuing a meal at a maintenance company's location. The famous *Gulaschkanone*—"goulash cannon"—can be seen to the right. Due to a shortage of purpose-built military vehicles, civilian ones were often impressed into service, as can be seen by the bus to the viewer's left.

Even the field bakery was hard at work—occasionally, it successfully joined in the fight against groups of scattered Bolsheviks. As part of the rear-area services, each division had a butcher company and a bakery company.

The uniform section also followed the forces in the field everywhere they went. It was completely "motorized," as the electric sewing machine demonstrates. Each company had an informal "tailor," and the battalion's usually had one listed on their tables of organization and equipment. The company tailor mended garments and also did custom work, which often explains some of the completely non-regulation uniforms seen in contemporary photography.

As a result of their uninterrupted and responsible duties, the maintenance companies keep the vehicles of the division in constant readiness. While that may have been true initially, the ever-lengthening supply lines of communication and the often bewildering array of vehicles employed in the divisions combined to make high percentages of vehicular readiness an almost impossible task. The bins seen here contain replacement parts for vehicles.

A welder in a tank maintenance company at work.

The eye of the army: The reconnaissance flight. It creates the supporting documents for new operations. Each armored division had a reconnaissance flight attached to it from the *Luftwaffe*. The most common aircraft used for reconnaissance duties was the ubiquitous Fieseler *Storch* ("Stork"), which was used in that capacity and many others until the end of the war.

The images from the new attack sector are evaluated.

Generaloberst Guderian arrives at a command post to discuss the situation prior to the start of a new offensive.

CHAPTER 14

On the Way to Roslawl in a Tank

IMPRESSIONS FROM A GREAT DAY OF VICTORY

Occasionally, the wind blew the repugnant smell of rotting horseflesh into the tank. The impacts of bombs had created seas of craters in the marshland next to the bridge. Crosses with helmets on them next to the road, signposts of the avenue of advance. Jutting out of a hole in the ground was the tail section with the Red Star of a shot-down Russian fighter. Your gaze extended across wide fields to the woods, which always came back up to the roads again. Wild and impenetrable.

In front of a deep depression, where engineers were still building a bridge, was a detour that headed out into the land. At that point, it was imperative to only move in the tracks ahead of you: minefield! In a small village, women and girls carried heavy bundles and their possessions to their impoverished root cellars—holes in the ground near their huts. The fear of an air attack by the Soviets, which had already sent a few villages up in flames, drove them to take those steps.

In the evening, the skies took on enormous dimensions. The black flag of smoke on the horizon lost its shape and form. In its place, a red shimmer emerged: Roslawl. The glowing flames shot ever higher into the growing darkness. A prime mover had to pull us through a sandy depression. Most of the vehicles got stuck there.

We then continued on with a motorcycle messenger. The night remained cast in the spell of the glowing mountain of flame over the rubble of the city. We got ever closer, so much so that we were blinded when we looked into the glowing hearth. The night remained irresistible within the magic circle of the fire, just as all eyes were drawn from a gigantic auditorium towards the small center of the stage. Our tanks were positioned behind the houses of the last village, looking like animals secretly crouched to jump, smelling prey. Their silent shadows must have had an effect on the primitive people of the village, as if armored creatures from the realm of the demons had surfaced. The tankers, however, well aware of their power, sat patiently on their "mythological creatures," killing time. Their black silhouettes stood out against the red horizon.

That night before the attack played out like a myth. All around, the silent shadows of the tanks in the abandoned village . . . the dark roundness of the horizon with the broad, high, serrated fiery gap . . . the smoldering and glowing beams with those confident men in the midst of them, for whom everything seemed subservient—the beauty of the night, the darkness, the fire, the steely armored animals and all of the future.

A couple of short hours of sleep in a foxhole. One of the steel monsters was parked above it. The hole, which had been dug by the ejected enemy, had been positioned poorly. It was just a portion of the shallow roadside ditch. Three of us slept together, with the *Oberstleutnant* in the middle. But we woke up abruptly, when our boots and pants were suddenly filled with water. A cloudburst had collected water in the ditch and turned our hole into a lake. We cursed . . . we laughed. It was just as well that the clock showed two and we had to get up anyway.

Orders, messengers, maps. The men turned over the engines on their tanks. There was a drumming in the palely arriving morning. One after the other, the reports that the elements were ready arrived.

There was a good mood in our tank. It was the tank commander's birthday. He was congratulated with heartfelt good wishes and a bottle of cognac was passed around in the narrow comradely confines of the tank. It warmed us up—especially good since we had to start the day with wet clothes. As a result of the sudden rain, the attack had been delayed somewhat. Motorcycle infantry and riflemen, drenched to the bone and encrusted with dreck from the road, moved through the cornfields, heavily laden with rain. Tanks rolled past. "Armed" with umbrellas, the tank commanders observed out of their cupolas. That conjured up a hearty laugh from those of us who were drenched.

The first enemy artillery fire. The waves of riflemen advanced. Motorcycles swarmed between the tanks. For us, the world broke down into the narrow slits of the vision ports and the few frequencies that the radio brought to our ears and mouths. But all of the guns were oriented. The excitement of the hunt came over us.

We moved across the fields in the direction of the city of Roslawl. The end could take us up in his sights from his cover and good visibility. All of a sudden, our vehicle received a dull blow. It trembled . . . it stopped . . . it burned. A direct hit from a light antiaircraft weapon. Everyone out! Was everyone able to get out? Thank God—yes! Attempts to put out the fire with fire extinguishers and sand were in vain. Wrapped up in a flag of smoke, our tank remained where it was.

We went to another tank and advanced to the southern edge of the city, establishing a blocking position. A fleeing column was engaged on the road. The biggest spectacle, however, was a shot of flame that arced powerfully skyward, appearing to seemingly go through the clouds and lose itself in the vastness. It was a fuel depot that had gone up in flames.

Blown-up bridges at the edge of the city. At one location was a ford that our tanks could wade through. The city had been softened up for the assault, and there was only occasional isolated resistance. The riflemen penetrated into the city. We rolled in after them.

Burned-out rows of houses. The first inhabitants started crawling out of their holes and started to plunder—avarice thrived in the shadows of the hard fighting. The war had so many faces! But our attack objective had been taken. Our next worry was to round up something for our hunger and our burning thirst. After all, new orders would arrive soon and, with them, new missions.

Stackpole Military History Series

Real battles. Real soldiers. Real stories.

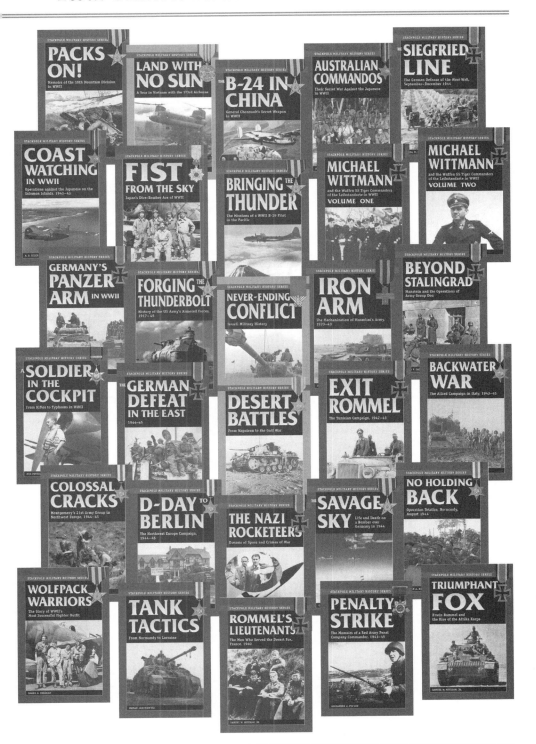

Stackpole Military History Series

Real battles. Real soldiers. Real stories.

Stackpole Military History Series

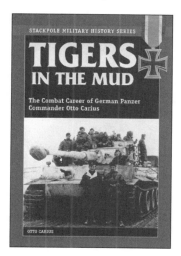

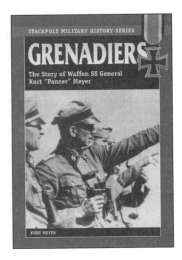

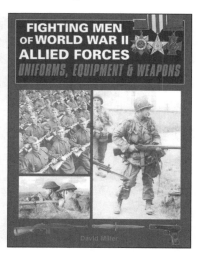